THE CAMBRIDGE BIBLE COMMENTARY

NEW ENGLISH BIBLE

GENERAL EDITORS

P. R. ACKROYD, A. R. C. LEANEY,
J. W. PACKER

THE WISDOM OF
SOLOMON

THE WISDOM OF
SOLOMON

COMMENTARY BY

ERNEST G. CLARKE

*Professor of Near Eastern
Studies, Victoria College, University of Toronto*

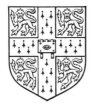

CAMBRIDGE

AT THE UNIVERSITY PRESS

1973

Published by the Syndics of the Cambridge University Press
Bentley House, 200 Euston Road, London NW1 2DB
American Branch: 32 East 57th Street, New York, N.Y.10022

© Cambridge University Press 1973

ISBNS:

0 521 08635 3   hard covers
0 521 09756 8   paperback

Printed in Great Britain
at the University Printing House, Cambridge
(Brooke Crutchley, University Printer)

GENERAL EDITORS' PREFACE

The aim of this series is to provide the text of the New English Bible closely linked to a commentary in which the results of modern scholarship are made available to the general reader. Teachers and young people have been especially kept in mind. The commentators have been asked to assume no specialized theological knowledge, and no knowledge of Greek and Hebrew. Bare references to other literature and multiple references to other parts of the Bible have been avoided. Actual quotations have been given as often as possible.

The completion of the New Testament part of the series in 1967 provides a basis upon which the production of the much larger Old Testament and Apocrypha series can be undertaken. The welcome accorded to the series has been an encouragement to the editors to follow the same general pattern, and an attempt has been made to take account of criticisms which have been offered. One necessary change is the inclusion of the translators' footnotes since in the Old Testament these are more extensive, and essential for the understanding of the text.

Within the severe limits imposed by the size and scope of the series, each commentator will attempt to set out the main findings of recent biblical scholarship and to describe the historical background to the text. The main theological issues will also be critically discussed.

Much attention has been given to the form of the volumes. The aim is to produce books each of which will be read consecutively from first to last page. The introductory material leads naturally into the text, which itself leads into the alternating sections of the commentary.

The series is accompanied by three volumes of a more general character. *Understanding the Old Testament* sets out to provide the larger historical and archaeological background, to say something about the life and thought of the people of the Old Testament, and to answer the question 'Why should we study the Old Testament?'. *The Making of the Old Testament* is concerned with the formation of the books of the Old Testament and Apocrypha in the context of the ancient near eastern world, and with the ways in which these books have come down to us in the life of the Jewish and Christian communities. *Old Testament Illustrations* contains maps, diagrams and photographs with an explanatory text. These three volumes are designed to provide material helpful to the understanding of the individual books and their commentaries, but they are also prepared so as to be of use quite independently.

P. R. A.
A. R. C. L.
J. W. P.

EDITOR'S PREFACE

To read The Wisdom of Solomon is like standing on a bridge. The book drew heavily on the Old Testament while hinting at ideas to be developed in the New Testament. The writer was also trying to bridge the distance between the ideas of the Old Testament and the ideas of the very different world in which he was living. We are still on that bridge because this book of Wisdom is really very new and contemporary in its significance as I hope the reader will find in this commentary.

I wish to express my thanks to the three General Editors of the series for inviting me to contribute a volume on Wisdom and for their continued advice and support. My family have listened patiently to many aspects of the growth of Wisdom and have offered many helpful suggestions.

The basic research was completed while on a sabbatical year in Cambridge, England – a year made most enjoyable by the kindness and friendship of the President, John Morrison, and Fellows of University College; and of Professor John Emerton. Finally, to the staff of the Cambridge University Press who have made it possible for this commentary to see the light of day, I am exceedingly grateful.   E. G. C.

CONTENTS

THE FOOTNOTES TO THE
N.E.B. TEXT

The footnotes to the N.E.B. text are designed to help the reader either to understand particular points of detail – the meaning of a name, the presence of a play upon words – or to give information about the actual text. Where the Hebrew text appears to be erroneous, or there is doubt about its precise meaning, it may be necessary to turn to manuscripts which offer a different wording, or to ancient translations of the text which may suggest a better reading, or to offer a new explanation based upon conjecture. In such cases, the footnotes supply very briefly an indication of the evidence, and whether the solution proposed is one that is regarded as possible or as probable. Various abbreviations are used in the footnotes.

(1) Some abbreviations are simply of terms used in explaining a point: *ch(s)*., chapter(s); *cp*., compare; *lit*., literally; *mng*., meaning; *MS(S)*., manuscript(s), i.e. Hebrew manuscript(s), unless otherwise stated; *om*., omit(s); *or*, indicating an alternative interpretation; *poss*., possible; *prob*., probable; *rdg*., reading; *Vs(s)*., Version(s).

(2) Other abbreviations indicate sources of information from which better interpretations or readings may be obtained.

Aq.   Aquila, a Greek translator of the Old Testament (perhaps about A.D. 130) characterized by great literalness.

Aram.   Aramaic – may refer to the text in this language (used in parts of Ezra and Daniel), or to the meaning of an Aramaic word. Aramaic belongs to the same language family as Hebrew, and is known from about 1000 B.C. over a wide area of the Middle East, including Palestine.

Heb.   Hebrew – may refer to the Hebrew text or may indicate the literal meaning of the Hebrew word.

Josephus   Flavius Josephus (A.D. 37/8–about 100), author of the *Jewish Antiquities*, a survey of the whole history of his people, directed partly at least to a non-Jewish audience, and of various other works, notably one on the *Jewish War* (that of A.D. 66–73) and a defence of Judaism (*Against Apion*).

Luc. Sept.   Lucian's recension of the Septuagint, an important edition made in Antioch in Syria about the end of the third century A.D.

Pesh.   Peshitta or Peshitto, the Syriac version of the Old Testament. Syriac is the name given chiefly to a form of Eastern Aramaic used by the Christian community. The translation varies in quality, and is at many points influenced by the Septuagint or the Targums.

Sam.   Samaritan Pentateuch – the form of the first five books of the Old Testament as used by the Samaritan community. It is written in Hebrew in a special form of the Old Hebrew script, and preserves an important form of the text, somewhat influenced by Samaritan ideas.

Scroll(s)   Scroll(s), commonly called the Dead Sea Scrolls, found at or near Qumran from 1947 onwards. These important manuscripts shed light on the state of the Hebrew text as it was developing in the last centuries B.C. and the first century A.D.

Sept.   Septuagint (meaning 'seventy'; often abbreviated as the Roman numeral LXX), the name given to the main Greek version of the Old Testament. According to tradition, the Pentateuch was translated in Egypt in the third century B.C. by 70 (or 72) translators, six from each tribe, but the precise nature of its origin and development is not fully known. It was intended to provide Greek-speaking Jews with a convenient translation. Subsequently it came to be much revered by the Christian community.

Symm.   Symmachus, another Greek translator of the Old Testament (beginning of the third century A.D.), who tried to combine literalness with good style. Both Lucian and Jerome viewed his version with favour.

Targ.   Targum, a name given to various Aramaic versions of the Old Testament, produced over a long period and eventually standardized, for the use of Aramaic-speaking Jews.

Theod.   Theodotion, the author of a revision of the Septuagint (probably second century A.D.), very dependent on the Hebrew text.

Vulg.   Vulgate, the most important Latin version of the Old Testament, produced by Jerome about A.D. 400, and the text most used throughout the Middle Ages in western Christianity.

[...]   In the text itself square brackets are used to indicate probably late additions to the Hebrew text.

(Fuller discussion of a number of these points may be found in *The Making of the Old Testament* in this series)

THE WISDOM OF SOLOMON

✳ ✳ ✳ ✳ ✳ ✳ ✳ ✳ ✳ ✳ ✳ ✳ ✳

THE TITLE

The title of this book, based on the original Greek, is intended
to indicate both the subject and the authorship. In the Septuagint it was placed among the wisdom books, between Job
and Ecclesiastes. As for the authorship, in ancient times it was
more important to have one's writing accepted than to get
personal recognition. Solomon was regarded as the fount of
all wisdom and was credited with being the author of the Old
Testament wisdom books. To assign the authorship of a book
to him ensured its acceptance. Furthermore, to assign the
writing to an ancient sage suggested its importance and indicated that its message was universal.

The question of whether Solomon had written it had
already been raised at an early date in the Old Latin Version,
the title of which was simply 'Book of Wisdom'. Some of
the early Church Fathers also rejected the tradition of Solomon's authorship. The title 'Wisdom' is more appropriate
since the theme of the book is wisdom's importance for
everyman and since it was written long after Solomon's time.

THE DATE AND AUTHORSHIP OF THE BOOK

Neither the language nor the content of the book gives any
hint to the date and authorship, except in the broadest terms.
Since the author used the Septuagint version of Old Testament
books, such as Job and Isaiah, he must have composed his book
some time after those books were translated into Greek (after

200 B.C.). Since he chose to write under Solomon's name rather than his own he probably lived earlier than Philo (20 B.C.–A.D. 45), the Jewish scholar of Alexandria, who used his own name. Also the ideas of this book are earlier than Philo, who developed concepts which are found here only in seminal form. Most scholars date the book to the mid-second or early first century B.C.

Although Solomon is said to be the author his name is mentioned nowhere in the whole book; only 'I' is found. Scholars have naturally tried to identify the author. All efforts in that direction, however, have failed. The fact that we do not know the author's name in no way lessens the validity of the message but allows us to concentrate on the meaning of the thoughts so eloquently presented.

The strong semitic flavour of the writer's Greek suggests that he must have been a hellenistic Jew, pious, and loyal to the Jewish law, who lived in Egypt – possibly in Alexandria. There was already a long tradition in that city of the blending of Jewish and Greek cultures, best expressed perhaps in the Septuagint. He was a member of that intellectual and cultured group of hellenistic Jews who had been educated in both traditions. He was equally at home in the poetic and philosophical writings of the Greeks and in the books of the Jewish Bible. Although conversant with current hellenistic ideas he held on to his Jewish faith, stressing that belief in God's sole sovereignty was the central focus for a meaningful life. He repudiated those ungodly Jews who lived only for the moment. He spoke of the Law of Moses as 'the imperishable light of the law' (18: 4). He regarded the representation of natural objects, common in the art of the hellenistic world, as impious if not insane (14: 18–21; 15: 4–6). He considered idolatry to be the source of all moral and social evil. In all this, the writer of Wisdom was a Hebrew of the Hebrews.

Scholars disagree on almost every subject concerning this book, including the question whether it was written by one or

2

more authors. As we shall see, however, both in purpose and language there is a genuine inner unity. And so we assume one Alexandrian Jew to be the author.

THE UNITY OF THE BOOK

There have been many scholars who have said that chs. 1–9 and 10–19 could not have been written by the same man because there are too many striking linguistic differences, especially in the choice of words. These differences, however, are superficial. For instance, the word 'wisdom' appears often in chs. 1–9 but is mentioned only three times in chs. 10–19. Furthermore, in 1–9 the topic is the life of the individual, but in 10–19 it is a philosophy of national history. On the other hand, the German scholar C. L. W. Grimm as long ago as 1860 presented equally strong arguments for the one-author theory. Many of the unusual Greek words and expressions appear in both sections. The spontaneity of the style and the richness of expression are the same throughout. Proper names are missing in the relevant sections of both parts. And, most significantly, there is an underlying unity of thought and purpose concerning human destiny and history in the whole book.

But although only one author wrote it, he may have used many different sources. The polemic against idolatry (13–15) and the prayer (9) may well have been already in existence. Such extra sources enrich the ideas of the book.

If the question of the author(s) has been a source of contention so also has been the question of the subdivisions in the book. In the main, however, we find four subdivisions which have different themes but could not stand independent of each other. But it is hard to determine the actual beginning and end of each subdivision because the conclusion to one section usually serves as the introduction to the next.

The following is suggested as a useful division of the several sections. Chs. 1–5 deal with the role of wisdom in man's destiny and compare the fate of the righteous and ungodly during this life and after. Chs. 6–9 discuss the origin and nature of wisdom and how it is to be found. In this section the author writes in the first person. Chs. 10–12 and 16–19 deal with the part played by God (and wisdom) in the history of the chosen people in one single event – the deliverance from bondage in Egypt. Inserted within this historical survey are chs. 13–15 – an integral part of 10–19 – which discuss the evils of idolatry.

THE PURPOSE OF THE BOOK

Primarily the writer directed his words to his fellow Jews but quite possibly he also thought of proselytizing the Greeks among whom he lived. The rulers to whom the author wrote are not the political rulers but everyman, who is created in God's image and has been given dominion over the world.

In a way, even to see the text as being addressed to the Jews living in Egypt is too narrow an interpretation. Frequently the writer began a section with a specific reference, e.g. to kings (1: 1; 6: 1), only to develop the thought in a more general way by applying the words to everyman (1: 3 'men'; 9: 13 'any man'). Likewise he referred to the Egyptians and the ungodly, or the faithful Jews and the godly, in such a way that a specific term becomes the general. Although the book begins as a treatise on a specific historical event, the exodus from Egypt, the writer transcended that historical situation and made it real in terms of the conditions among the exiles in Egypt in his own day.

Specifically, then, the readers to whom the book was addressed may be subdivided into two groups. First, there were those fellow Jews who had abandoned the faith of their fathers (2: 12) and had been attracted to the cultural life of the Greeks with its imposing philosophical systems, its advanced knowledge in the physical sciences, astrology, the occult, the plastic arts, the sensuous. He hoped to rekindle within them a genuine zeal for God and the law by showing that Judaism need not take second place to anything in hellenism (chs. 1–9) and that there was a chosen destiny for the Jewish people (18: 4 'the imperishable light of the law was to be given to the world'). Furthermore, he sought to prepare them, as well-educated Jews, to live in a hellenistic society; to provide religious insights, in a contemporary form, in order to establish links between their traditional faith and all the new ideas of the pagan society wherein they lived.

As well as these, the author probably had in mind another group of fellow Jews: those who, although they had remained faithful, were perplexed and disheartened by disappointment, ridicule, and persecution (2: 10–12, 17–20). For them the book is a well-reasoned argument which would encourage and reinforce their faith (chs. 10–12; 16–19).

In addition to these two groups, the author may have intended his words for gentile readers. Judaism is a religion that aims at making converts and Jews always hoped that non-Jews would hear and turn to God. The Gentiles they had in mind would be those well-educated Greeks who could understand the Jewish arguments when they were couched in Greek terms. The writer wanted to show that the Jew was not a barbarian. He showed his God, unlike the Greek idols who were the product of the Greeks' own imagination, as merciful and, as the creator of the world, worthy of worship. We should stress, however, that, although the writer did not exclude the Gentile, his first concern was to sustain his fellow Jews in the faith of the fathers and to encourage them to keep in mind their chosen destiny as rulers of the world.

Within the purposes stated above the writer was also able to compare Greek and Jewish intellectual forces and to show the genuine integrity and vitality of Judaism in contrast to the bankruptcy of hellenistic materialism and idolatry. No matter how much human wisdom a man acquired, it was only through the gift of divine wisdom that he could really fulfil his true destiny of living with God, even though, like all men, he must experience physical death. Only with God's gracious gift could man set all the limiting features of this earthly life in their proper perspective.

LANGUAGE AND LITERARY STYLE

In the Apocrypha there are only two books which deal with wisdom: this one and Ecclesiasticus. This one, which is the later in date, differs in style from all the other wisdom books of the Old Testament. Instead of grouping ideas in small units around a common theme, Wisdom provides a sustained logic of argument which was made possible under the influence of Greek literary form. The author has expressed his thoroughly Jewish theological position in the form of rhetoric which was so popular with his contemporaries in Egypt. This made it possible for him to develop a style of persuasive teaching in which the unity of the message was presented through a diversity of literary forms such as a monologue (chs. 1–5), a personal open letter written in the first person (chs. 6–9), a speculative treatise on such questions as man's final destiny, the origins and evils of idolatry (chs. 13–15), the question of authority, etc.

Although some scholars have argued that the earlier chapters, at least, must have been first written in Hebrew and then translated into Greek it seems more likely that the book was written in Greek originally. For one thing Greek was the language of the readers to whom the author addressed his writings and they would be familiar with Greek thought-patterns and literary forms. The Jews to whom he addressed this book had turned to hellenistic culture and might not have been ready to receive a message couched in the Jewish biblical language alone.

There are other reasons for arguing that the original was in Greek. The spontaneous style, the subtle play on words, and the unique Greek vocabulary would be difficult to maintain in translation. Some of the Greek philosophical and technical terms are without a ready Hebrew counterpart. There are 335 Greek words not found in the Septuagint: this suggests that the author was familiar with other Greek writings.

At the same time it is understandable that some scholars should argue that Wisdom was first written in Hebrew. The author did not use Greek expressions indiscriminately but filled them with Hebrew thoughts. He kept his independence and used only those Greek expressions and ideas which would assist his efforts to prove that the Jewish culture and religion were still a valid way of life and need not be rejected for the more popular philosophical and religious movements of the day. Indeed the writer's response to this challenge demonstrates his original genius and the depth of his faith. He contemplated the marvels of God's revelation in history and then related it to the advances in contemporary science to produce an argument for the divine plan of salvation for mankind.

There are many instances where the form is Greek, most often based on the Septuagint, but the idea itself remains Hebraic. An example is the use of the Greek word 'to visit' in the semitic sense of both 'punishment' (14: 11 – N.E.B. 'fall upon'; 19: 15 – N.E.B. 'a judgement') and 'blessing' (2: 20 – N.E.B. 'protector'; 3: 7 – N.E.B. 'coming'; 4: 15 – N.E.B. 'comes'). Also the Hebrew literary form known as 'parallelism' in the poetry is very much in evidence. By this is meant the balancing of synonymous expressions in one of several different ways. For instance in 1: 2–4 'those who trust'/'those who never doubt'; 'will not enter'/'make her home'; 'shifty soul'/'body that is mortgaged to sin' are parallels expressing two aspects of a single idea. Sometimes, as in 2: 16, the parallels help explain each other ('base coin'/'as if we were filth'). At other places the parallelism is contrasting ('outrage'/'patience'; 'torment'/'forbearance' (2: 19)). It is regrettable that the N.E.B. has rendered the Greek poetry into prose because often it is very difficult to identify the parallelism and hence part of the author's literary style is lost. Certainly the

7

Hebrew poetic form was an important part of the author's literary expression.

There are also a number of Hebrew expressions translated directly into Greek, such as 'you rulers of the earth' (1: 1); 'discipline' in the sense of education (1: 5); 'inmost being' and 'heart' for feelings and thoughts (1: 6); 'vigilant ear' for God (1: 10); 'in God's hand' in the sense of protection (3: 1); 'abominations' for idols (12: 23).

KEY IDEAS

The writer's plan of attack was to present his Jewish ideas on wisdom in terms of the hellenistic civilization in which he was educated and in which he lived in order to satisfy the needs and expectations of his readers. The style and literary allusions he employed suggest that his readers were familiar with Greek literature and philosophy. At no time, however, did he compromise his Jewish faith by the terms he used. Indeed just the opposite was true. He used the Greek language, its literary style and philosophical systems, to enhance his Jewish ideas, for his purpose was to prove that Judaism was the only true way of life. At the same time, as we shall note in the following paragraphs, the writer was expressing his views in a context somewhat alien to Judaism, which resulted in a significant step forward in the history of ideas. His approach was dynamic, creative, and more universal than any earlier biblical writer.

The writer's use of the basic Old Testament belief that the beginning of wisdom is the worship (fear) of God is a good example of this (ch. 1; cp. Prov. 1: 7). He made use of the idea in his criticism of the shortcomings of hellenism, especially nature-worship (13: 1–9). Such nature-worship was the epitome of philosophical religion but it made for a mistaken understanding of creation. Nature and all the things of life were simply means, not ends. They aided man in fulfilling his final destiny but they were not that final destiny.

Wisdom is a way of thinking. The wise men of the Old

Testament were the humanists of Israel and as such were valuable critics of a too rigid institutionalism. The wise men approached fundamental questions through observation and experience rather than by abstract speculation. The basic single difference between the wise men of the Old Testament and Greek philosophers was that the former began with the premise 'in the beginning God...' and 'the beginning of wisdom is the fear of God'. They believed in God and were, therefore, no atheists. The Greek philosophers questioned everything, even the existence of God. In Wisdom it is man's relationship with God and man's role during his time on earth that are questioned.

As for the theological views of the book it should be stressed that the writer was neither a theologian nor a philosopher. He was not making a systematic theological statement of fundamental Jewish beliefs. Rather, as already noted, he was a man with a deep faith that the Jewish God was the supreme God who ordered all things. Consequently, the doctrine of God in this book describes his nature rather than asks the question whether he exists or not.

In a way, the God of Wisdom is the traditional God of the Jews. He is the all-powerful creator of the universe, the ruler of destiny. He manifests himself in various forms as 'power' (1: 3), the 'vigilant ear' (1: 10), 'spirit' (1: 7), 'hand' (7: 16), 'almighty Word' (18: 15) but primarily as 'wisdom'. He is merciful and just, always relating the punishment to the sin (12: 15–18). He desires man's life not his death (1: 14; 2: 23) so that even the punishment of the Egyptians is tempered with the hope for their repentance (ch. 12). In discussing the nature of God the writer drew least on Greek ideas and terminology.

When we turn to consider Wisdom's anthropology or views on the nature of man, we are again in the midst of an examination of Greek terms, familiar to his readers, but used in a semitic or Old Testament sense. The main words are 'body' and 'soul'. They appear in 1: 4; 8: 19–20; 9: 15. Two other passages (11: 17; 15: 11) are indirectly relevant to the discussion. Commentators have taken great pains to establish whether or not the writer was really influenced by, and dependent directly upon, the Greek philosophy of Plato. Rather we should begin by noting that the writer used these two words as expressing the two essential aspects of a total human being, much as Gen. 2: 7 where it is stated that God breathed his spirit into the newly moulded body and it became a living person. Furthermore, the writer believed that God's creation was good (Gen. 1: 10, 12, etc.) and that 'he created all things that they might have being' (1: 14). Even the 'formless matter' (11: 17) out of which God created the world does not suggest sin or evil. It is man who has introduced evil through his ignorance of God's true purpose for him.

In 1: 4 the stress is not on any sinfulness of the body or shiftiness of the soul but on the total man's capacity to become sinful. Wisdom will not dwell in a sinner. Hence there is no contradiction between 'noble soul' and 'unblemished body' (8: 19–20).

The verses 8: 19–20 are a parenthesis within the argument that man, even though he has acquired all human wisdom, is limited without the gift of divine wisdom, for which he must pray. After a description of the physical birth of everyman (7: 1–6) these verses develop the idea that the personality resides in the soul rather than in the body alone as expressed in the Old Testament. At the same time he did not fully accept the Greek idea of the pre-existence of the soul. His concept is closer to 15: 11 – 'inspired him with an active soul and breathed into him the breath of life' (cp. Gen. 2: 7). The subtle balance between the Hebrew and the Greek thought demonstrates the writer's genius.

The final key passage in Wisdom's anthropology is 9: 15, where 'perishable body' is an explanation, not of sin, but of the physical limitations of man. Such an admission is appropriate in the prayer of a perfect man, i.e. a man of 'noble soul' and 'unblemished body', who realizes that he needs still more: the gift of divine wisdom.

Key ideas

In all these passages, then, the writer was striving to prove that there is more to living than this mortal, restrictive life which all men live. He was impelled to discuss immortality while acknowledging that by nature man is mortal: 'all come into life by a single path, and by a single path go out again' (7: 6). In actual fact this is the fate of both the just and the ungodly. However, for the just, death is not the end of man, because man is created incorrupt (2: 23 'immortality') and by seeking wisdom and justice becomes immortal. On the other hand, for the ungodly, the fact that by nature man was mortal meant that life was merely 'A passing shadow' (2: 5).

From this it seems plain that immortality is not the immortality of the soul in the Greek sense of the pre-existence of the soul. Although some scholars have argued that the Greek philosophical view of the immortality of the soul was the basis for Wisdom's ideas, it was not, even though it quite possibly provided the climate of thought in which the writer could take his own step forward. The writer's view that personality resided in the soul (8: 19–20) was a logical extension of the Hebrew ideas on life after death, which were treated in a very limited way in the Old Testament.

The first fact to observe is that the word 'immortal' is never used with the idea of life/soul in Wisdom. It always refers to something which happens to man or some aspect of his relationship to God. It is man's 'hope' (3: 4), 'remembrance' of him (4: 1), his kinship with wisdom (8: 13, 17), his doing justice (1: 15) and righteousness (15: 3) which is immortal. The fundamental aspect of man's immortality is expressed in the idea that he was created, by nature, incorrupt (2: 23 'immortality'). To keep God's laws is a warrant of incorruption (6: 18 'immortality') for the light of the law itself is incorrupt (18: 4 'imperishable') as is also the spirit of God which abides in all men (12: 1 'imperishable'). Both law and spirit are aids to keep man close to God. The writer was here speaking of a positive quality that man was endowed with at creation rather than of a goal man could strive for. It is kingship naturally endowed.

Secondly, it should be noted, by contrast, that man is to be 'mortal' (7: 1; 15: 17) and his idols also (14: 8 'perishable thing'). His body is 'mortal' (9: 15 'perishable') and his ability to reason also (9: 14 'feeble').

Thirdly, there are passages where life/soul is connected with life and death but in these instances it has the Hebraic sense of person not the Greek sense of soul: 'the souls of the just' (3: 1), 'the great assize of souls' (3: 13), and 'His soul was pleasing' (4: 14).

There is no resurrection of the body mentioned in this book; also the final overthrow of the wicked will take place on this earth (4: 20 – 5: 14).

In 6: 17–21 we observe the steps that everyman must take to obtain immortality. Wisdom alone is the means. And so we can understand that even though man is incorrupt by nature, wisdom's assistance in achieving immortality (expressed in the prayer in ch. 9) is essential if a man is to live a justly righteous life. The enjoyment of immortality depends upon God's power to give life back to man, and not merely on his power to save man from death. If man rejects God's gift then, through ignorance of the true nature of God, he gets death.

✳   ✳   ✳   ✳   ✳   ✳   ✳   ✳   ✳   ✳   ✳   ✳   ✳

The promise of immortality

SEEK GOD AND AVOID EVIL

1 LOVE JUSTICE, you rulers of the earth; set your mind upon the Lord, as is your duty, and seek him in sim-
2 plicity of heart; for he is found by those who trust him without question, and makes himself known to those who
3 never doubt him. Dishonest thinking cuts men off from God, and if fools will take liberties with his power, he

shows them up for what they are. Wisdom will not enter 4
a shifty soul, nor make her home in a body that is mortgaged to sin. This holy spirit of discipline will have nothing 5
to do with falsehood; she cannot stay in the presence of
unreason, and will throw up her case at the approach of
injustice. Wisdom is a spirit devoted to man's good, and 6
she will not hold a blasphemer blameless for his words,
because God is a witness of his inmost being, who sees
clear into his heart and hears every word he says. For the 7
spirit of the Lord fills the whole earth, and that which
holds all things together is well aware of what men say.
Hence no man can utter injustice and not be found out, 8
nor will justice overlook him when she passes sentence.
The devices of a godless man will be brought to account, 9
and a report of his words will come before the Lord as
proof of his iniquity; no muttered syllable escapes that 10
vigilant ear. Beware, then, of futile grumbling, and avoid 11
all bitter words; for even a secret whisper will not go un-
heeded, and a lying tongue is a man's destruction. Do not 12
stray from the path of life and so court death; do not draw
disaster on yourselves by your own actions. For God did 13
not make death, and takes no pleasure in the destruction of
any living thing; he created all things that they might 14
have being. The creative forces of the world make for
life; there is no deadly poison in them. Death is not king
on earth, for justice is immortal.   15

* The Old Testament states (Prov. 1: 7) that 'the fear of the
LORD is the beginning of knowledge' and that 'fools scorn
wisdom and discipline'. The author of Wisdom developed
these two ideas in 1: 1–15 and 1: 16 – 2: 24.

The first idea, presented in 1: 1–15, offers immortality to the man who pursues 'justice' (1: 1) because it alone is 'immortal' (1: 15). Here is the essence of the book.

In these verses, man is exhorted to love justice because wisdom will not enter a perverse soul, because the spirit of God fills the whole earth, and because in the last analysis God intended man to live, not die.

The argument is somewhat complex because the author used several different terms to express the various manifestations of God: 'justice' (1: 8); 'power' (3); 'wisdom' (4); 'spirit' (7); 'vigilant ear' (10). At the same time wisdom which becomes the main manifestation of God is spoken of as a 'holy spirit of discipline' (5). The net result of these several terms, however, is always reference to God.

The verses are subdivided as follows: 1–3, rulers of the earth are urged to search out God; 4–7, it is said that wisdom will aid man in his pursuit of her; 9–11, it is said that the unjust man will be cut off; 12–15, man is urged to avoid death since it is not part of God's design for him.

1–3. Although the author began the book by addressing his remarks to the *rulers of the earth*, he soon centred his exhortation on man. By contrast, in 6: 17–21, the argument begins with an appeal to man to seek wisdom and thereby obtain 'kingly stature'. The phrase *rulers of the earth* (originating in the Septuagint of Ps. 2: 10) is more fully explained as 'kings', 'lords of the wide world' (6: 1), 'rulers of the multitude' (6: 2), 'viceroys of his kingly power' (6: 4) and 'rulers of the nations' (6: 21). Those who assumed Solomon to be the author have argued that he is addressing his fellow-rulers. If *earth* is synonymous with 'country' the author was addressing the Roman rulers who inflicted severe suffering on the Jews of Alexandria. Others argue that the author has in mind the Jewish rulers of Alexandria who had renounced their religion. Probably it is simply a rhetorical device to hide the real purpose: warning and encouragement to the Jews living in Egypt. Certainly the real subject of the book is everyman. In the Old Testament man is crowned with honour and dignity, called to have dominion, and to be in every sense a king (Ps. 8). In this book man is called to rule God's creation as 'steward of the world in holiness and righteousness' (9: 3) and to share in the everlasting kingship with God (5: 16; 6: 21). Therefore in the phrase *rulers of the earth* the author summarized the meaning of Gen. 1: 26, 'man in our image and likeness to rule...'

It is unnecessary, therefore, to attempt an identification of the phrase *rulers of the earth*. The author was speaking to everyman and urged him to

(1) *Love justice*; a phrase drawn from David's prayer in 1 Chron. 29: 17 ('plain honesty pleases thee'). *justice*, appearing eleven times in Wisdom; here and 1: 15; 5: 18; 12: 16; 2: 11 and 14: 7 (translated 'right' in the N.E.B.); 5: 6 (translated 'truth' in the N.E.B.); 8: 7 (twice – 'virtue' and 'justice'); 9: 3 and 15: 3 (translated 'righteousness'), is all-important because it is 'immortal' (1: 15; 15: 3). It teaches the cardinal virtues of 'temperance and prudence, justice and fortitude' (8: 7). In Hebrew the word means what is right, just, normal, and is used to describe the actions both of God and man. Both aspects are found here. The thought is paralleled in the rest of the verse and suggests that *justice* is God, an idea developed by the later rabbis. At the same time, in the light of the other instances in the book, *justice* means man thinking and acting in harmony with God, and showing this in his relations with his fellowmen. As such it is the opposite of wickedness;

(2) *set your mind upon the Lord, as is your duty*: the Greek of this phrase means 'fairmindedness' without reservation, as a servant would give his master full attention (Eph. 6: 5);

(3) *seek him in simplicity of heart*: as in 1 Chron. 29: 17 the simple-hearted man has a singleness of purpose; no other allegiance than the central one of searching out wisdom (cp. 6: 15). The *Dishonest* man is the opposite, and is perverse (cp. 11: 15; 19: 3). The reason for the strong threefold

exhortation is that God has no patience with the perverse who trifle with him (*his power* – a contemporary substitute for the word God). The use of the imperative in this verse means that man is to act, not just speculate. Such exhortation is common in the Bible where the prophets and the wise men urge man to seek God (Amos 5: 5) and the 'kingdom' (Matt. 6: 33). The reward in Wisdom, of course, is eternal life with God (5: 15).

4–5. A number of manuscripts have substituted 'discipline', which is a variant in the Bible, for the word 'Wisdom'. 'Wisdom' and 'discipline' are regularly linked in parallel construction because they are integrally related with the ultimate task of knowing God and obtaining immortality (cp. Ecclus. 6: 18 'wisdom's discipline'). In addition, 'Wisdom' is also called 'a spirit' (verse 6) and 'holy' (7: 22). Although 'wisdom', 'spirit' and 'holy' are synonyms, the idea of God manifesting himself as wisdom is the one to persist and to be most fully developed in chs. 1–10 of the book.

In summary, then, God is wisdom and 'this holy spirit of discipline' is wisdom (verse 5) and 'wisdom is a spirit' (verse 6), therefore God as spirit 'fills the whole earth' (verse 7).

4. *shifty soul...body that is mortgaged to sin*: the Greek word translated by *shifty* is rare biblically and comes from the verb meaning 'to act fraudulently' or 'to deceive'. The idea is well suited if the reference is to those Jewish leaders of Alexandria who have renounced their religion. However, since everyman is the main topic it is the evildoers of ch. 2 who are being described. From this verse one ought not to deduce that the body is the source of moral evil nor argue for the inherent wickedness of the flesh.

The parallel phrasing with *soul* and *body* does not suggest two distinct entities but rather expresses the idea of a total person. Hence we may paraphrase the verse: divine wisdom will not enter into a sinful man. In Hebraic thought man is a unity and the words 'body' and 'soul' are synonyms expressing this idea and do not suggest the Greek idea of man as

16

made up of distinct parts: body, soul, spirit. Therefore divine wisdom dwells in both soul and body at the same time.

Furthermore, the definition of soul as *shifty* and the body as *mortgaged to sin* shows that neither the body nor the soul was the unique source of sin. In fact, 1: 4 is merely stating in a philosophical way the ethical thought of 1: 3, 5. The only distinction which may exist in this verse is the suggestion that there are spiritual sins and physical sins. *mortgaged to sin* finds its fullest development in John 8: 34 'everyone who commits sin is a slave' and in Rom. 7: 14–25 in such phrases as 'purchased slave of sin' and 'a slave to the law of sin'.

5. *This holy spirit of discipline*: the stress on *This* in the N.E.B. indicates that wisdom is itself the *holy spirit of discipline*, although the Greek is different. The phrase as a synonym for wisdom is at the same time a synonym for God who is 'holy spirit' (9: 17). *holy spirit* is a personification of God already found in the Greek Bible (Isa. 63: 10–11). *unreason* is dishonest thinking (1: 3; cp. 4: 11 'falsehood'; 14: 25 'fraud') as also in the parallel *falsehood* and *injustice*. The origin of wisdom (7: 25–6) as 'a pure effluence from the glory of the Almighty' suggests why wisdom *cannot stay*. The extent of the abhorrence which wisdom has for evil is expressed in the verbs: *cannot stay* and *will throw up her case*.

6. *Wisdom is a spirit devoted to man's good*: the Greek 'loving man' (7: 23 'kindly towards men'; 12: 19 'kind-hearted') is a very apt epithet and very much in vogue in the hellenistic literature of the period but is not found in the Septuagint and only three times in the New Testament. It was a quality expected in every ruler of the day. The word was the writer's answer to the charge that the Jews were 'unsocial', i.e. not devoted to the good of their fellowmen. Proverbs (8: 17ff.) speaks of wisdom endowing with riches and filling the treasuries of those who seek her. *a blasphemer*: i.e., one who reviles God as described in 2: 1–20. This hellenistic Greek word in classical times meant simply 'evil speaking'. *God is a witness of his inmost being, who sees clear into his heart and hears every word*

he says: God is *episcopos* (*sees clear*). Elsewhere in the Septuagint the word means 'taskmaster' or 'captain'. The Old Latin has *scrutator*, i.e. 'inspector' or 'examiner'. The *inmost being* is where passions and subconscious impulses originate (cp. Ps. 16: 7 'wisdom comes to me in my inward parts') and the *heart* is the source of ideas, while *every word he says* (in the Greek 'his tongue') gives expression to those thoughts. And God will most intensely take note of the blasphemer's tongue. The reference to the three parts of man's person are essential to indicate the degree to which God is involved in man's thinking process.

7. *For the spirit of the Lord fills the whole earth*: cp. 11: 26 – 12: 1. The omnipresence of God as spirit is the basis for the assertion of the preceding verse. Does the *spirit of the Lord* mean God or wisdom? In the Old Testament 'the spirit of God' is God in his activity in the world; and, as such, is omniscient and omnipresent. The phrase (in the second half of the verse), *that which holds all things together*, is borrowed from Greek philosophical thought of a divine bond which unified the world. Here the author of Wisdom sets it parallel to *the spirit of the Lord* and so emphasizes the fact that it is God's spirit which is the unifying force in the world. *that which... is well aware of what men say* is God who has the 'vigilant ear' (1: 10). The author of Wisdom continued to emphasize the concept of God, manifest in the world of man, as power, wisdom and spirit. There is a fluidity in the author's thinking as there is in the Old Testament generally concerning God and his various manifestations. The one constant factor is that God is absolute and the several manifestations are only extensions of his personality. In this period the synonym for God which dominated, but in no sense negated, the others was wisdom.

8–11. Since God's spirit 'fills the whole earth' (verse 7) man's injustice will be uncovered and God as justice will act. The word *Hence* provides the link in the argument between 1: 4–7 and what follows.

8. *justice*: still another personification of God (cp. 11: 20)

which as expressed in the Septuagint is the idea of God taking vengeance on the sinner. *overlook*: the Greek word, used five times (here and at 2: 7 'escape'; 5: 14 'passed on'; 6: 22 'leave untold'; 10: 8 'ignored'), conveys the sense of the Hebrew word 'to forgive' as expressed by the rabbis.

9. *The devices...brought to account...report of his words... proof of his iniquity*: *devices* means craftiness; *report of his words* – according to Jewish tradition a book of remembrance was kept to record all man's good and bad deeds. In Mal. 3: 16 a 'record was written'. The imagery in verses 9–10 is of a ruler who keeps watch on all the thinking and doing of his subjects.

10–11. God is that ruler with a *vigilant ear*. The phrases *muttered syllable...lying tongue* express the dissatisfaction found in man; e.g. *bitter words* in Greek means 'to speak against God', an idea which comes close to blasphemy (1: 6). All this leads to *a man's destruction*. In the light of 4: 20 it may be assumed that the author did not here intend the total annihilation of the wicked. However, 3: 18–19 suggests that the unjust generation has 'a hard fate in store for it' (cp. 4: 19; 5: 1–5; 12: 27; 19: 1). The rabbis taught that the souls of the righteous went straight to God, while those of the wicked wandered to and fro, chased by angels, but not annihilated.

12–15. The idea of these verses expressed in the phrase 'the destruction of any living thing' (verse 13) brings us close to the author's idea of immortality. It is through the Septuagint of Prov. 8: 35–6 that our author found the common ground between the hellenistic terms and the Hebraic ideas he sought to express.

12. *Do not stray from the path of life and so court death*: while the wicked are in limbo the righteous are urged to seek God and obtain his favour. The Greek word *court* is a very strong one and, for instance, was used to describe seeking admission to one of the religious sects of the day. What kind of death is Wisdom speaking of in these verses? We note the following reasons for interpreting *death* as spiritual. (1) There was no

19

doubt about a physical death and mortal decay in that day (9: 15). (2) There is no reference in this book to the actual death of the wicked but simply to the state of limbo (4: 19–20; 5: 1–5). (3) In 1: 11 it is said that the 'lying tongue is a man's destruction'. (4) The emphasis, and to some extent the key to the argument of 1: 12–15 if not to the whole book, is the quite spiritual idea that 'justice is immortal' (1: 15). The doctrine of immortality being put forward is not the immortality of the soul because of its nature, but the immortality of the righteous because they follow justice, which is God, who is immortal. The righteous, by loving God (justice), are above mortal death but not free of it. As noted, the word immortal is never used with soul.

13. *For God did not make death*: the author stated here quite categorically why man is urged to seek justice and thereby immortality. We may ask then: whence come evil and death? Although man's body is mortal (9: 15; 11: 17; see p. 11) and all men must die physically yet, in the Hebrew view, God took no pleasure in the death of a man. Indeed our author stated that man was made for immortality (1: 4; 2: 23; 11: 24–6) because God's incorrupt spirit is in all things (12: 1). In 14: 6–8 the argument for saving Noah was that he might bring forth 'a new breed of men'. In fact the argument here suggests absolute free-will as expressed in Deut. 30: 19 'I offer you the choice of life or death, blessing or curse. Choose life.'

On the other hand, when Wisdom speaks of death, it intends spiritual death. Such death entered the world by 'the devil's spite' (2: 24). In contrast to the immortality promised the righteous, death to the sinful man is not only physical death but also spiritual death.

14. *created all things that they might have being*: to partake of God's essential beingness. Again the basis for the idea is found in the Hebrew 'to be' which conveys the sense of being, becoming, existing. *The creative forces of the world make for life*: the Greek word for *creative forces* offers several possible interpretations attested in the Septuagint and Apocrypha. Here the phrase

means either 'races of creatures' or 'generative powers'. The rabbinic view was that the *creative forces* only became harmful when Adam lost his immortality by sin and, with the Fall, the earth produced poisonous insects and reptiles. The Greek word for 'life' was common in the writer's day, to convey the idea that life goes on for mankind through succeeding generations of creatures. The combination of these two ideas emphasizes God's concern to keep the world going. In Greek philosophical thought the argument is that God creates the ideas but that matter escapes the control of deity.

15. *Death is not king on earth*: the Greek text reads 'the palace of Hades is not upon earth' suggesting possibly that Sheol is the royal palace of Hades. Although the N.E.B. has paraphrased the original text, it underlines the idea that what is meant is not the resting place of the dead but the power of death personified. In the Old Testament death and Hades are identical and often the two words are joined. The sense is in accord with the statement that 'God did not make death' (1: 13). *for justice is immortal*: in this phrase we find the culmination of the argument concerning man's true destiny and it can be summarized: love justice, for justice is immortal. The idea of this verse is expanded in 15: 3 where the power of the saving God is the root of immortality. According to Prov. 3: 18 wisdom is called 'a staff of life'. Having argued, therefore, that *justice is immortal* (cp. 5: 15; 6: 17–20; 8: 17) the first step to that immortality is the discovery of God who is justice. In Jer. 9: 23–4 the argument is that man should not glory in anything except the knowledge of God who is kind, just, and righteous. *

THE WAY OF THE UNGODLY

But godless men by their words and deeds have asked 16 death for his company. Thinking him their friend, they have made a pact with him because they are fit members of his party; and so they have wasted away.

2   They said to themselves in their deluded way: 'Our
life is short and full of trouble, and when a man comes to
his end there is no remedy; no man was ever known to
2 return from the grave. By mere chance were we born,
and afterwards we shall be as though we had never been,
for the breath in our nostrils is but a wisp of smoke; our
reason is a mere spark kept alive by the beating of our
3 hearts, and when that goes out, our body will turn to
ashes and the breath of our life disperse like empty air.
4 Our names will be forgotten with the passing of time, and
no one will remember anything we did. Our life will
blow over like the last vestige of a cloud; and as a mist is
chased away by the sun's rays and overborne by its heat,
5 so will it too be dispersed. A passing shadow – such is our
life, and there is no postponement of our end; man's fate
6 is sealed, and none returns. Come then, let us enjoy the
good things while we can, and make full use of the
7 creation, with all the eagerness of youth. Let us have costly
wines and perfumes to our heart's content, and let no
8 flower of spring escape us. Let us crown ourselves with
9 rosebuds before they can wither. Let none of us miss his
share of the good things that are ours; who cares what
traces our revelry leaves behind? This is the life for us; it
is our birthright.'

✳ 16. This verse belongs with ch. 2 and states the thesis of the
section. The author has so arranged it in order to underline the
sharp contrast between him who loves justice (ch. 1) and
godless men who both in *words* (2: 1–9) and *deeds* (2: 10–20)
associate themselves with death. As we shall see, their argument
is based on delusion (2: 1, 21). The seriousness of their wilfulness is expressed in this verse by a threefold se tof relation-

ships. Death is treated as a welcome companion. They make a covenant with death because *they are fit members of his party.* Finally, they pine for death. The N.E.B. *wasted away* fails to convey fully the idea of lust which is implied in the Greek word.

2: 1–5. A statement of the current ideas about mortal man. The description is valid and one to which even the author of this book subscribed although he did not understand physical death to be the end of the relationship with God.

1. For the ungodly, however, there is no *remedy* at the end of his life. The word *remedy* is open to one of two interpretations: (1) with Eccles. 8:8 the idea would be that there is no escaping the end by any man which is the sense of the argument here as seen in verse 5; (2) the Vulgate reads 'rest' suggesting that not even at man's end is there a cure for his earthly troubles. 4: 19–20 states that the ungodly will be in anguish while in 4: 7 the author argues that the righteous are 'at rest' even in 'an untimely death'. Because the ungodly see nothing but emptiness in life they argue as the first part of the thesis (2: 6–9) that man should live this materialistic life to the full without any care for what is left behind. In fact it is their 'birthright' (2: 9).

2–5. What is man like according to the ungodly? He was born by *mere chance.* Certain contemporary Greek philosophers also subscribed to this idea, suggesting that man was merely a random combination of atoms. This materialistic view of man is expressed in such phrases as *the breath in our nostrils is but a wisp of smoke, reason is a mere spark kept alive by the beating of our hearts, our body will turn to ashes, the breath of our life* will dissolve in the air, and *Our names will be forgotten.* The same arguments are forcefully presented in Ecclesiastes.

Man's life is as a passing cloud and a shadow, and man cannot postpone the end because time moves on inexorably. For the Hebrews once the breath or spirit had departed, life was at an end. The crux of the argument is how one interprets this irrefutable fact of life. The position which the ungodly take in 2: 6–9 is based on biblical passages such as are found in Ecclesiastes. Contrast this with the view expressed in 1: 1, 15.

6–9. The first conclusion drawn by the ungodly in their thesis about the mortality of man. The ideas expressed here stress a completely materialistic world: they want (1) *the good things* which are immediately at hand (*while we can*) rather than imaginary pleasures of the future; (2) the *share of the good things* (verse 9) which are rightfully theirs. The argument here is reminiscent of the exhortation by Eccles. (2: 24) to eat, drink and enjoy life which is God's gift. ✶

DOWN WITH POOR AND HONEST MAN!

10 'Down with the poor and honest man! Let us tread him under foot; let us show no mercy to the widow and
11 no reverence to the grey hairs of old age. For us let might
12 be right! Weakness is proved to be good for nothing. Let us lay a trap for the just man; he stands in our way, a check to us at every turn; he girds at us as law-breakers,
13 and calls us traitors to our upbringing. He knows God, so he says; he styles himself "the servant[a] of the Lord".
14, 15 He is a living condemnation of all our ideas. The very sight of him is an affliction to us, because his life is not like
16 other people's, and his ways are different. He rejects us like base coin, and avoids us and our ways as if we were filth; he says that the just die happy, and boasts that God
17 is his father. Let us test the truth of his words, let us see
18 what will happen to him in the end; for if the just man is God's son, God will stretch out a hand to him and save
19 him from the clutches of his enemies. Outrage and torment are the means to try him with, to measure his
20 forbearance and learn how long his patience lasts. Let us

[a] *Or* child.

24

condemn him to a shameful death, for on his own showing he will have a protector.'

So they argued, and very wrong they were; blinded by 21
their own malevolence, they did not understand God's 22
hidden plan; they never expected that holiness of life
would have its recompense; they thought that innocence
had no reward. But God created man for immortality, 23
and made him the image of his own eternal self; it was 24
the devil's spite that brought death into the world, and
the experience of it is reserved for those who take his side.

✳ 10–20: the ungodly present the second part of their thesis:
oppress the weak and the righteous. Here, the just man is the
object of the ungodly's attack. The reason for the ungodly
wanting to *lay a trap* for the righteous (verse 12) and to *test the
truth of his words* (verse 17) is twofold: first, the righteous are
a living condemnation of the ungodly (verse 14). The righteous
reproach (*he girds at*, verse 12) the ungodly *as law-breakers* who
reject the Law of Moses (cp. 6: 18) and as *traitors to* their *upbringing* who do not observe the religious traditions of their
faith (cp. 6: 17 'desire to learn'). In other words, these are the
apostate Jews. Furthermore, the ungodly feel that the righteous reject them as *base coin*, an idea explained by the word *filth*
(verse 16) in the parallel line. The ungodly argue, falsely, that
to get rid of the *affliction* (verse 15), of the sight of the righteous,
would make all well. In verse 16 the Greek behind the
phrase *the just die happy* suggests that the ungodly seek the
punishment of the righteous in the latter part of life, i.e. in this
life and not after death, which is in keeping with their view of
mortal man.

The second and more fundamental reason for the ungodly
to *test* the righteous is to challenge God to vindicate the righteous (*in the end*, verse 17) rather than merely to seek vengeance
on man himself. The just man *knows God…styles himself* 'the

servant of the Lord' (verse 13), *boasts that God is his father* (verse 16) and *protector* (verse 20). The righteous themselves have argued (*on his own showing*, verse 20) that God will be their *protector*. The semitic idea behind this word contains the sense of both protection and examination. Contrary to what some scholars assert, the line of argument in these verses indicates the idea of protection.

The basis for the righteous man's confidence in ch. 2 is that he is *God's son*. The author was consistent in his imagery, interchanging 'child' and *son*. Therefore in verse 13 the word 'child' in the footnote is preferable to *servant* – a Hebrew word often translated by the Greek for 'child' in the Septuagint. 'child' *of the Lord* (verse 13) and *God's son* (verse 18) are synonyms.

To some extent the filial relationship which the righteous have with God is the last straw. The ungodly decide to test the seriousness of God's relationship by *outrage* (insult) and by *torment* (torture) of the righteous (verse 19). The persecution of pious Jews was very common in the hellenistic world.

We may well ask: who were *the righteous* and *the ungodly*? Those who argue that the book is addressed to the wicked apostate rulers find proof in verses such as 2: 10. However, it is more likely that the ungodly in general is intended, since the writer spoke of a class being persecuted, not individuals. Likewise he was not referring to a specific period but drawing on the experience of the persecution of the righteous in such Old Testament passages as those concerning the suffering servant in Isaiah (cp. Isa. 52: 13 – 53: 12).

The Church Fathers found in this passage a prophecy of Christ's passion. There are indeed significant coincidences such as Matt. 27: 43 ('let God rescue him, if he wants him – for he said he was God's Son'). However, the similarities are due to the same Old Testament passages serving as the basis of this book and of the New Testament. No Christian would have written of Christ's passion in such terms without some reference to the resurrection.

21-2. These verses contain the book's evaluation of the two

arguments put forward by the ungodly. Such views as those expressed in 2: 6–20 are due to not knowing God's purpose (22) and not understanding man's true destiny (verses 23–4). The author of Wisdom made it quite clear that, although being blind to spiritual things was the result of wickedness, the cause of that wickedness was the inability of the ungodly to accept that he was created for a fellowship with God which would transcend death, even though man is mortal.

God's hidden plan: the mystery of God is not a doctrine of immortality that is only for the initiated but God's purpose for the righteous on earth (4: 17). The ungodly never thought there was to be *recompense* for the holy life; an idea Wisdom develops in chs. 3–4.

23–24. Exactly parallel to the thought in 1: 12–15. Man is immortal because he is made in the *image* of God's *own eternal self*. Although *image* is a Platonic term, the background of the idea is found in the 'image of God' expression of Gen. 1: 26–7. In 7: 26 wisdom is described as the image of God's goodness.

Consequently, since it was God's purpose that man should be immortal, why does man experience death? In such passages as 2: 23 (cp. 1: 13) Wisdom stresses that the universe is entirely good and filled with the spirit of God and denies either that God made death or that he intended it to be the inevitable end of man's life. It is man, destined for immortality through virtue and wisdom (1: 15; 2: 22; 6: 18; 8: 17; 15: 3), who takes the side of the devil (24) by joining his party (1: 16).

There are two views as to how death entered the world: either through Cain's murder of Abel or by the envy of the serpent in the Garden. In the Septuagint 'devil' translates the Hebrew 'Satan'. The first instance in the Old Testament where 'Satan' is portrayed as man's tempter is in 1 Chron. 21: 1 when 'Satan' incited David to take a census. In Wisdom, for the first time, *devil* is substituted for 'Satan' in reference to Gen. 3 and the serpent's tempting of man.

Wisdom nowhere suggests a dualism, because there is one God whose supremacy is never questioned. *the devil's spite* is not against God but against man who is created in the *image* of God. Death is physical death, which is an intruder (1: 12–14). Man will *experience* death in the same way that he will experience God's judgement (12: 26) if he does not heed God's admonition. The corollary of death for the ungodly is immortality for the righteous. What kind of immortality? This subject Wisdom takes up next when we read 'the souls of the just are in God's hand' (3: 1). ✳

REWARDS AND PUNISHMENTS

✳ In two contrasting sections in ch. 3 the author developed further the thesis that life belongs to the righteous (1–9) and death to the ungodly (10–19). As in chs. 1–2 he discussed what he meant by immortality in terms of reward ('torment shall not...' 3: 1) and 'punishment' (3: 10). In both this chapter and the next the argument is based on the belief that the ungodly did not understand 'God's hidden plan' (2: 22). Central to Jewish thought on reward and punishment is the belief that God's blessing is demonstrated in (1) a life without suffering, (2) many children, and (3) a long life. Wisdom takes up these three topics in order to show that suffering (3: 2ff.) may be part of God's plan, that childlessness (3: 13–14; 4: 1–6) may be a blessing, and that premature death (3: 17–18; 4: 7–20) may be the fate of the righteous. ✳

3 But the souls of the just are in God's hand, and torment
2 shall not touch them. In the eyes of foolish men they
   seemed to be dead; their departure was reckoned as
3 defeat, and their going from us as disaster. But they are
4 at peace, for though in the sight of men they may be
5 punished, they have a sure hope of immortality; and after
   a little chastisement they will receive great blessings,
   because God has tested them and found them worthy to
6 be his. Like gold in a crucible he put them to the proof,

and found them acceptable like an offering burnt whole
upon the altar. In the moment of God's coming to them 7
they will kindle into flame, like sparks that sweep through
stubble; they will be judges and rulers over the nations of 8
the world, and the Lord shall be their king for ever and
ever. Those who have put their trust in him shall under- 9
stand that he is true, and the faithful shall attend upon him
in love; they are his chosen, and grace and mercy shall be
theirs.

✻ 1–4. Although the ungodly consider (*seemed, reckoned as,
in the sight of men*) that the suffering which the righteous
are experiencing is punitive (*dead, defeat, disaster, punished*)
it actually was cleansing (*great blessings*) in God's eyes. Therefore, the chapter begins with a positive statement: *the just are
in God's hand, and torment shall not touch them.*

souls of the just: in the Hebrew sense of the total person;
not of a soul distinct from the body. It is the use of a part to
represent the whole. Hence the phrase suggests no distinction
between body and soul but is another way of saying 'the just'.
God's hand: in God's power for protection. *torment...*:
although it could be the suffering of the body that is meant
(2: 19), more likely it is the anguish after death (4: 19), since
that is exactly what the wicked suffer, while the just escape it.
It may also be that the author of Wisdom intended to contrast
the 'torment' meted out by the ungodly to the righteous (2: 19)
in this life with that experienced by the wicked after death.
foolish men, called 'frivolous' in 3: 12, are ignorant of the true
facts. *they seemed to be dead; their departure was reckoned as
defeat, and their going from us as disaster* suggests the way the
ungodly looked at the death of the just. The writer did not
deny the death of the just but suggested that in death the just
have gained three significant qualities: (1) *peace* (verse 3) – the
Old Testament idea of peace in the neutral sense of rest in the

grave (Isa. 57: 2 'enter into peace...rest in their last beds')
while here the idea is of the just being at ease because of the
hope of immortality; (2) *sure hope of immortality* (verse 4): although in the Greek *sure* can modify either *hope* or *immortality*,
the N.E.B. stresses the surety of the hope, rather than the
guarantee of immortality, because *the just are in God's hand*. In
contrast, the hope of the ungodly is 'void' (3: 11); (3) 'great
blessings' (see below on verse 5).

The term *immortality* appears often in Wisdom (2: 23;
6: 18–19) but never in the Greek Old Testament. Furthermore, the term is never used with 'soul' in Wisdom because
in this book immortality is thought of in earthly terms. The
idea is somewhat mystical. Therefore, it is difficult to cate-
gorize Wisdom's thinking on the subject too rigidly. The
difficulty is due to the author's facility in appropriating Greek
terms that do not properly belong to his own Jewish way of
thinking. Immortality, for Wisdom, is not dependent on any
Greek idea of the pre-existence of the soul before it entered
a human body. Wisdom is speaking of mankind rather than
the resurrection of the individual body. Without denying that
man is 'mortal' (7: 1), with 'a perishable body' (9: 15), the
writer stressed that it is his character rather than his nature
which determines whether he lives or dies (see pp. 10–12).
Immortality is at the same time man's moral achievement and
God's gracious gift through his spirit. Furthermore, this immortality is personal and not the immortality that is achieved
by having descendants (4: 1).

The man who loves justice gets immortality, not so much
through living on after death in some undefined way, as
through being immortal because justice and wisdom are time-
less. *immortality*, therefore, describes the destiny for which God
ordained man (2: 23); the hope of the righteous (here); that
which wisdom imparts to those who love and follow her
(6: 18, 19; 8: 13, 17); the result of acknowledging God to be
the whole of righteousness (15: 3); the memory of virtue
(4: 1; cp. 8: 13); the spirit of God and of law (12: 1; 18: 4).

5–6. *great blessings* is the third benefit (see above) that the just receive. *little chastisement*: *little* means not of long duration; *chastisement* is instruction, which is a frequent theme in Wisdom (6: 25). It includes being tested in order to prove one's worth. Even God's chosen must be so chastened (a theme developed in chs. 10ff.) but not like God's enemies who are scourged ten thousand times more (12: 2). Testing is a biblical concept: in Gen. 22: 1 Abraham was tested; in Exod. 15: 25 the children of Israel were tested at Marah. These verses are the key to verses 1–9 and emphasize that the suffering of the righteous is cathartic and not punitive. The righteous are tested and not found to be base as are the ungodly (2: 16). *worthy to be his* and *acceptable like an offering burnt whole upon the altar* refer to the value of the righteous in contrast to the wicked.

7–9. The principal messianic passage of the book. Although some have considered that the passage referred to a specific 'judgement' event it is better to understand it along with 5: 1–14 as describing the inevitability of judgement for the wicked and of reward for the righteous without trying to work out the time and place. Wisdom is concerned with the idea of judgement, not with when it happens. *In the moment*: not a specific time but the idea that God will come in his own time. Likewise 'the great assize of souls' (3: 13), 'at the end' (3: 17), and 'in the hour of judgement' (3: 18) do not refer to specific time. *God's coming*: cp. p. 26, where we noted that the Hebrew root has two meanings. Here the meaning is the protection of the righteous, because the Lord shall be their king and he is true. *they will kindle into flame, like sparks that sweep*... refers to the righteous and their final victory. *like sparks* suggests brightness and swiftness. Kindling into flame is a metaphorical way of saying they will be exalted as *judges and rulers*. But although the righteous will rule *the nations*, God is *their king*. The origin of this idea is Ps. 10: 16 ('The LORD is king for ever and ever') but Wisdom has added *their* to emphasize that only *his chosen* are in 'God's hand' (verse 1). ✳

10 But the godless shall meet with the punishment their evil thoughts deserve, because they took no account of 11 justice and rebelled against the Lord. Wretched indeed is he who thinks nothing of wisdom and discipline; such men's hopes are void, their labours unprofitable, their 12 actions futile; their wives are frivolous, their children 13 criminal, their parenthood is under a curse. No, blessed is the childless woman if she is innocent, if she has never slept with a man in sin; at the great assize of souls she shall 14 find a fruitfulness of her own. Blessed is the eunuch, if he has never done anything against the law and never harboured a wicked thought against the Lord; he shall receive special favour in return for his faith, and a place in the 15 Lord's temple to delight his heart the more. Honest work bears glorious fruit, and wisdom grows from roots that 16 are imperishable. But the children of adultery are like fruit that never ripens; they have sprung from a lawless 17 union, and will come to nothing. Even if they attain length of life, they will be of no account, and at the end 18 their old age will be without honour. If they die young, they will have no hope, no consolation in the hour of judge- 19 ment; the unjust generation has a hard fate in store for it.

✳ 10–19. These verses are part of a larger unit (3: 10 – 4: 20) in which the writer condemned the way of the ungodly by refuting the idea that children and long life were proof of God's blessing. 'Punishment' (verse 10) is called the 'full weight of divine judgement' (12: 26) and is deserved. This is the punishment-to-fit-the-crime thesis which frequently appears in the second half of the book.

10–11. The godless expressed evil thoughts when they (1) *took no account of justice*, which one was advised to pursue if one wanted immortality; (2) *rebelled against the Lord*; (3) gave no thought to *wisdom* (the essence of justice) nor to *discipline* (the path leading to justice). Consequently the ungodly find their lives *wretched*. Their hope is *void* in contrast to the righteous man's hope (3:4).

12–14. The term *frivolous* is used often to describe the ungodly (3: 2 'foolish'; 5: 4; 15: 5 'fools'; 11: 15 'insensate'; 12: 24 'thoughtless children').

parenthood is under a curse despite the traditional view that children are a blessing ('Sons are a gift from the Lord...happy is the man who has his quiver full of them', Ps. 127: 3, 5). Consequently in verses 13–14 the *childless woman* and the *eunuch* are most blessed. *childless woman*: a barren married woman, not a celibate. There is no crime here if she is *innocent*, i.e. has not slept with another man. *eunuch*: according to Isa. 56: 4–5 he is a worthy member of the community, contrary to the view of Deut. 23: 1 which forbade a eunuch to enter the congregation. In Matt. 19: 12 three types of eunuchs are mentioned: those who are so from birth, those who are made so by men, those who are so by choice. Wisdom considers the first two as the phrase *never done anything against the law* makes clear. Matthew's third category would be unacceptable since there is no argument in Wisdom for celibacy or asceticism. Sterility of the pure is not a matter for reproach: it results in *fruitfulness of her own* for the woman and *special favour* and *a place in the Lord's temple* for the eunuch. This last phrase, based on Isa. 56: 5, is very likely an answer to Deut. 23: 1.

15. This concludes the argument of 13–14 by equating *honest work* with those qualities of faithfulness found in the childless woman and the eunuch. Good works produce *glorious fruit* and roots of wisdom. The same argument is found in rabbinic writings: a man who dies childless regrets the fact. God replies that the man has 'fruit more beautiful than children', namely, 'the Torah of which it is written (Prov. 11: 30): "the fruit of righteousness is a tree of life"'. Rabbinic exegesis developed the thesis that the 'fruit of the

righteous' is good deeds not children. Here, the synonymous pairs are *Honest work* and *roots that are imperishable*; *glorious fruit* and *wisdom* (prudence; cp. 8: 6, p. 57).

16. *But* emphasizes the contrast with verses 13–15. *children of adultery...sprung from a lawless union* is presented here in contrast to verse 15. The idea is based on Isa. 57: 3–5 which argues that adultery is unfaithfulness to God and results in producing bastard children. Furthermore, *like fruit that never ripens...will come to nothing* is contrasted with the argument that faithfulness and honest work produce glorious fruits. Although the writer might well have been referring to apostate Jews, it is more likely that he was thinking universally.

17–18. Wisdom challenges the traditional view of what the length of one's life means. Whether 'the children of adultery' live long or die young they will be *without honour* and *have no hope*. Contrary to Jeremiah's and Ezekiel's ideas about individual responsibility, Wisdom is arguing here for a doctrine of hereditary sin (although modified in 12: 23).

19. *a hard fate* is in store for the unjust generation in contrast to the fate of the just in verse 1. The idea of *hard* is expanded in 4: 1–6. *fate* denotes finality: the term is in the same category as 'at the end' and 'in the hour of judgement'. ✻

THE GOOD MAN IS VIRTUOUS

4 It is better to be childless, provided one is virtuous; for virtue held in remembrance is a kind of immortality, because it wins recognition from God, and from men too.
2 They follow the good man's example while it is with them, and when it is gone they mourn its loss; and through all time virtue makes its triumphal progress, crowned with victory in the contest for prizes that nothing can
3 tarnish. But the swarming progeny of the wicked will come to no good; none of their bastard offshoots will

strike deep root or take firm hold. For a time their 4
branches may flourish, but as they have no sure footing
they will be shaken by the wind, and by the violence of
the winds uprooted. Their boughs will be snapped off 5
half-grown, and their fruit will be worthless, unripe,
uneatable, and good for nothing. Children engendered in 6
unlawful union are living evidence of their parents' sin
when God brings them to account.

But the good man, even if he dies an untimely death, 7
will be at rest. For it is not length of life and number of 8
years which bring the honour due to age; if men have 9
understanding, they have grey hairs enough, and an unspotted life is the true ripeness of age. There was once such 10
a man who pleased God, and God accepted him and took
him while still living from among sinful men. He was 11
snatched away before his mind could be perverted by
wickedness or his soul deceived by falsehood (because 12
evil is like witchcraft: it dims the radiance of good, and
the waywardness of desire unsettles an innocent mind);
in a short time he came to the perfection of a full span of 13
years. His soul was pleasing to the Lord, who removed 14
him early from a wicked world. The mass of men see this 15
and give it no thought; they do not lay to heart this truth,
that those whom God has chosen enjoy his grace and
mercy, and that he comes to the help of his holy people.
Even after his death the just man will shame the godless 16
who are still alive; youth come quickly to perfection will
shame the man grown old in sin. Men will see the wise 17
man's end, without understanding what the Lord had
purposed for him and why he took him into safe keeping;
they will see it and make light of him, but it is they whom 18

the Lord will laugh to scorn. In death their bodies will be dishonoured, and among the dead they will be an object

19 of contempt for ever; for he shall strike them speechless, fling them headlong, shake them from their foundations, and make an utter desert of them; they shall be full of

20 anguish, and all memory of them shall perish. So in the day of reckoning for their sins, they will come cringing, convicted to their face by their lawless doings.

✳ Ch. 4 expands on the subject of children and life-span introduced in ch. 3 by contrasting the hope of the righteous (verses 1–6) with the fate of the ungodly (verses 7–20).

1–2. The justification of being *childless* is to be *virtuous*. In 3: 13 there is no condemnation for the childless woman provided she is 'innocent'. The writer meant, not celibacy, but childlessness from natural or accidental causes. *virtue held in remembrance is a kind of immortality* contradicts the more generally held view, as expressed in Eccles. 1: 11, that man is unremembered. It is true that Wisdom argues that the names of the ungodly will be forgotten (2: 4) but it claims that the righteous man *wins recognition* from both God and man and so is not forgotten. *virtue* (5: 13; 8: 7) is the key. This is an example of the writer using a Greek philosophical term in a biblical sense. In the light of 8: 7 it is obvious what Wisdom is really stating is that one must possess the four cardinal virtues of 'temperance and prudence, justice and fortitude', the presence of which is proved by good works. Virtues alone persist *through all time*. There is an air of victory invoked by the phrases *triumphal progress, crowned with victory, prizes that nothing can tarnish* (the fruitful life culminating in immortality).

3–6. *But* introduces the contrast in these verses of the fruitlessness of the ungodly's *progeny*. The idea finds some parallel in Ps. 1: 4–5: 'Wicked men...are like chaff driven by the wind ...shall not stand firm.' In the New Testament the parable of the seed falling on stony ground (Mark 4: 3ff.) and of the fig-

36

tree bearing no fruit (Mark 11: 13ff.) deal with the consequences of the fruitlessness of the ungodly life (cp. 3: 15). *God brings them to account – them* can refer to the children or the parents, but most likely both together (3: 12); *account* i.e. 'visitation', referring to the final judgement.

7–20. The third major aspect of Jewish retribution concerns premature death.

7. *But*: contrasting these verses with 3: 17–18 and 4: 3–6. *good man...untimely death...at rest*: the background for this idea is in Isa. 57: 1–2 'The righteous perish...no one cares ...but they enter into peace'.

8–9. Neither longevity nor premature death matter. All that matters is that *men have understanding* and *an unspotted life*. Wisdom is still referring to the idea found in 3: 15 and 4: 1. The emphasis is on quality, the inward character.

10–15. *once such a man*: the man who had the qualities mentioned in 7–9 is Enoch (cp. Gen. 5: 24 where the same vocabulary is used). It is a characteristic of Wisdom not to identify by name the examples cited. This is especially so in the second half of the book. Both Ecclesiasticus (49: 14) and Hebrews (11: 5) mention Enoch by name. Why then the anonymity in Wisdom? It is most likely that the writer assumed that the readers would recognize the references, since the examples cited are all typical.

11. *snatched away*: i.e. he miracuously disappeared to escape defilement; 'His soul was pleasing to the Lord, who removed him early from a wicked world' (verse 14) suggests the idea that the good die young.

12–13. Although verse 12 interrupts the Enoch theme it is relevant because it suggests that there are influences in the world which are too strong for even the innocent to bear. *evil is like witchcraft*, which suggests both the fascination working on the innocent but also the evil force of the agent (cp. 2: 24 'the devil's spite'); *waywardness of desire* is a unique Greek word coined by the author of Wisdom to convey the degree of perversion; *full span of years* is in contrast to the failure of the ungodly to mature (3: 16; 4: 5).

15. *The mass of men*: i.e. the majority of people, which may refer to the Gentiles and the heathen nations as well as to the apostate Jews; *give it no thought* (cp. verse 17 'without understanding') expresses the same indifference to and ignorance of the plight of the righteous as is found in ch. 2; *grace and mercy*: cp. 3:9; *comes to the help* is 'visitation' in the sense of watching over.

16. *Even after his death the just man will shame the godless who are still alive* does not refer to the final judgement but to the daily moral contrast between the honest work and virtuous life of the just man, which lives on as a remembrance; and the ungodly's own life which is dead, even though he is still alive.

17. This explains the reason for the 'shame' of verse 16. The ungodly do not understand what God *purposed* nor why he took them into *safe keeping* as he did Enoch.

18–20. The 'shame' of the ungodly is that (1) they will be laughed *to scorn* by God (Ps. 2:4 'The Lord who sits enthroned in heaven laughs them to scorn'); (2) *their bodies will be dishonoured*, i.e. left unburied (Isa. 66:24 'the dead bodies of those who have rebelled against me...abhorred by all mankind'); (3) they will be *an object of contempt for ever* (Ezek. 32:24 'men who struck terror into the land of the living but now share the disgrace of those that go down to the abyss'); (4) God *shall strike them speechless* in contrast to their earlier arrogance (verse 15); (5) he will *fling them headlong*, i.e. fling aside as a discard (Ps. 102:10 'In thy wrath...thou hast...flung me aside'); (6) he will *shake them from their foundations* as in an earthquake; (7) they will become *an utter desert*; (8) they will be *full of anguish* in contrast to the rest and peace of the just (3:1; 4:7); (9) *all memory of them shall perish*: the ungodly had already argued so in 2:4 but did not there think of it as punishment.

20. *in the day of reckoning*: i.e. the 'great assize of souls' (3:13), the bringing to 'account' (4:6). This is the introduction to the next chapter. ✳

THE JUST AND THE UNGODLY IN JUDGEMENT

Then the just man shall take his stand, full of assurance, **5**
to confront those who oppressed him and made light of
all his sufferings; at the sight of him there will be terror 2
and confusion, and they will be beside themselves to see
him so unexpectedly safe home. Filled with remorse, 3
groaning and gasping for breath, they will say among
themselves: 'Was not this the man who was once our
butt, a target for our contempt? Fools that we were, we 4
held his way of life to be madness and his end dishonour-
able. To think that he is now counted one of the sons of 5
God and assigned a place of his own among God's people!
How far we strayed from the road of truth! The lamp of 6
justice never gave us light, the sun never rose upon us.
We roamed to our heart's content along the paths of 7
wickedness and ruin, wandering through trackless deserts
and ignoring the Lord's highway. What good has our 8
pride done us? What can we show for all our wealth and
arrogance? All those things have passed by like a shadow, 9
like a messenger galloping by; like a ship that runs 10
through the surging sea, and when she has passed, not
a trace is to be found, no track of her keel among the
waves; or as when a bird flies through the air, there is no 11
sign of her passing, but with the stroke of her pinions she
lashes the insubstantial breeze and parts it with the whirr
and the rush of her beating wings, and so she passes
through it, and thereafter it bears no mark of her assault;
or as when an arrow is shot at a target, the air is parted 12
and instantly closes up again and no one can tell where it
passed through. So we too ceased to be, as soon as we 13

were born; we left no token of virtue behind, and in our
14 wickedness we frittered our lives away.' The hope of
a godless man is like down flying on the wind, like
spindrift swept before a storm and smoke which the wind
whirls away, or like the memory of a guest who stayed
for one day and passed on.

15   But the just live for ever; their reward is in the Lord's
16 keeping, and the Most High has them in his care. Therefore royal splendour shall be theirs, and a fair diadem from
the Lord himself; he will protect them with his right hand
17 and shield them with his arm. He will put on from head
to foot the armour of his wrath, and make all creation his
18 weapon against his enemies. With the cuirass of justice on
his breast, and on his head the helmet of doom inflexible,
19, 20 he will take holiness for his impenetrable shield and sharpen
his relentless anger for a sword; and his whole world shall
21 join him in the fight against his frenzied foes. The bolts of
his lightning shall fly straight on the mark, they shall leap
upon the target as if his bow in the clouds were drawn in
22 its full arc, and the artillery of his resentment shall let fly
a fury of hail. The waters of the sea shall rage over them,
23 and the rivers wash them relentlessly away; a great tempest will arise against them, and blow them away like
chaff before a whirlwind. So lawlessness will make the
whole world desolate, and active wickedness will over-
turn the thrones of princes.

* 'Then' (verse 1) is the 'day of reckoning' of 4: 20 which
will be a time of judging the ungodly. What kind of judgement is intended and when? Scholarly interpretation of this
chapter ranges all the way from a description of a judgement

scene after death to a poetic tableau of the late repentance of the sinner. The number of verses devoted to the subject would indicate its importance to the author. However, we note that the writer was more concerned with the state of the sinner's soul and the reasons why he has acted so than with specific punishment, in verses 1–14. Likewise, although rewards for the just are described (15–16) they are set within the context of God as armed warrior destroying his 'frenzied foes' (verses 17–23). The whole judgement scene is set in the context of eternity.

2–13. Most of the arguments advanced by the ungodly for their mockery of the just and their failure to understand the meaning of life have already been treated in chs. 2–4. Here, however, the idea is repeated in a universal context.

2. *unexpectedly safe home*: the idea of the unexpected runs throughout Wisdom. It conveys a sense of reversal and is therefore dramatic.

3. *Was not this the man who was once our butt, a target for our contempt?* (cp. ch. 2) – now the tables are turned.

5. *he is now counted one of the sons of God* (cp. 2: 18): while the ungodly admit that they are 'fools'. The idea of being *counted* is to be understood in the context of the Old Testament where men are kept in a book of life or erased from it as in Ps. 69: 28

> let them be blotted out from the book of life
> and not be enrolled among the righteous.

6. *road of truth*: i.e. the road which leads to truth. The ungodly admit that neither the *lamp of justice* nor *the sun* led them to learn God's true will. The ungodly do not deny the existence of such aids to truth but only confess to their own failure to use them because of 'pride...wealth and arrogance' (verse 8). This agrees with the thesis of ch. 2.

7. This verse states what the ungodly did instead: wandered *through trackless deserts* and ignored *the Lord's highway*.

9–12. A series of similes to describe the transient nature of the ungodly life. They are piled up to emphasize the writer's point. All the similes except that of the arrow are biblical.

According to Prov. 30: 19, 'the way of a vulture in the sky' and 'the way of a ship out at sea' are too wonderful for man to comprehend.

13. This introduces the conclusion to the five preceding similes and underlines the fact that life is so short that it seems that *we too ceased to be, as soon as we were born*. Because all their time was consumed in *wickedness* they *left no token of virtue*, i.e. good works (cp. 4: 1 'virtue...is a kind of immortality'). According to 2: 9 the ungodly do not care what trace their revelry leaves.

14. The author's summary of the ungodly man's life. *The hope of a godless man* is described by four similes to stress the argument in verses 9–13 that there is no trace of him left. There is probably no more pathetic image of transience than that of the stranger in the night or the traveller who spends each succeeding night in a different place ('O hope of Israel... must thou be a stranger in the land, a traveller pitching his tent for a night?' Jer. 14: 8).

15–16. *the just live for ever*: in contrast to the ungodly who leave no trace of virtue or hope. The argument of these verses builds on the ideas in verses 13–14. *for ever* is not literally an extension of time but an expression of the quality of the just man's life lived under God's protection. The synonyms *Lord's keeping* and *in his care* express the same idea, as already admitted by the ungodly (verses 5–13) in their conclusion that (1) the just will achieve *royal splendour*: i.e. they will share the kingdom, since 'death is not king' (1: 15); (2) they will have *a fair diadem*: i.e. be crowned with righteousness in contrast to the crowns of rosebuds put on the ungodly (2: 8); (3) God *will protect them...and shield them*: i.e. he will champion the just's cause.

17–23. The last idea of verse 16 ('shield') introduces the topic of the final judgement on God's 'frenzied foes', which is set in cosmic, apocalyptic terms. It is the idea of judgement itself which is being developed and not the details of an actual trial. Although the writer was forced to express his idea in specific terms, because of his Hebraic outlook, his main theme was the terror and magnitude of what God was about to do to the wicked.

Although many Old Testament passages may have influenced the writer, Isa. 59: 16–18 with such phrases as 'helmet of salvation', 'garments of vengeance', 'wreaking his anger on his foes', is most likely the direct influence. In Wisdom itself the same ideas are restated in 18: 14–16 and 19: 13–17. In the New Testament Eph. 6: 11–17 is written in the context of both the Old Testament and Wisdom passages.

In these verses the stages of judgement are effected, firstly, by the appearance of God as an earthly warrior properly clad for war (cp. 18: 15ff.): *armour of his wrath*: a zeal for the love of his chosen provokes God to action; *cuirass of justice*: breastplate; *helmet of doom inflexible*: judgement which is unswerving; *impenetrable shield*: God is so absolutely righteous that all argument against his decisions is useless; *relentless anger for a sword*: the word of God which condemns (cp. 18: 16ff.).

Secondly, God summons his whole creation against the wicked: *all creation* (verse 17), i.e. nature, a favourite idea with the writer (cp. 5: 21; 16: 17, 24; 19: 6); the *whole world* (verse 20) joins in battle against the *frenzied foes*: those who are blinded with madness like the fools in 5: 4–7.

Thirdly, God marshals natural forces to attack the enemy: *lightning, bow in the clouds, hail, waters of the sea, rivers, a great tempest, a whirlwind* are all familiar Old Testament instruments of punishment in God's arsenal. For instance, in Judg. 5: 20 'the stars in their courses fought against Sisera'. The use of nature in judgement shows us that the writer conceived of the punishment of the wicked in more than temporal terms.

23. The last sentence beginning *So lawlessness . . .* serves both to conclude chs. 1–5 and to introduce chs. 6–9. The two parts are parallel in idea in order to emphasize the degree of chaos which would ensue if lawlessness were given full reign. ✵

43

In praise of wisdom

✳ In a certain sense chs. 2–5 have been a descriptive diversion, concerning the just and the ungodly, from the initial exhortation 'love justice'. Since the way of the ungodly would leave no trace (2: 9; 5: 13), and 'the just live for ever', then (6: 1) it is obvious which way 'kings', that is, everyman, should act. Furthermore, wisdom will help man to 'love justice'. ✳

AN APPEAL TO RULERS TO LEARN WISDOM

✳ Ch. 6 is a closely argued statement on wisdom. It can be subdivided into two sections: 1–8 and 9–11; 12–21 and 22–5. ✳

6 HEAR THEN, YOU KINGS, take this to heart; learn
2 your lesson, lords of the wide world; lend your ears, you rulers of the multitude, whose pride is in the myriads
3 of your people. It is the Lord who gave you your authority; your power comes from the Most High. He will put your actions to the test and scrutinize your intentions.
4 Though you are viceroys of his kingly power, you have not been upright judges; you do not stand up for the law
5 or guide your steps by the will of God. Swiftly and terribly will he descend upon you, for judgement falls
6 relentlessly upon those in high place. The small man may find pity and forgiveness, but the powerful will be called
7 powerfully to account; for he who is all men's master is obsequious to none, and is not overawed by greatness. Small and great alike are of his making, and all are under
8 his providence equally, but it is the powerful for whom he
9 reserves the sternest inquisition. To you then who have

absolute power I speak, in hope that you may learn wisdom and not go astray; those who in holiness have kept 10 a holy course, will be accounted holy, and those who have learnt that lesson will be able to make their defence. Be 11 eager then to hear me, and long for my teaching; so you will learn.

✱ 1–4. As in ch. 1 the appeal to rulers is an appeal to everyman. *wide world* suggests that man has dominion over the whole earth of which he is the steward (*viceroys*). The stewardship with which man is entrusted is further qualified by indicating that the rulers have taken bribes (*not been upright judges*), associated with those who rejected the Mosaic Law (*do not stand up for the law*), and did not themselves submit to God's will (*guide your steps by the will of God*) from which everyman's *authority* and *power* stems (verse 3).

5–6. *judgement falls relentlessly*: those in authority might expect to escape being called to account. The author of Wisdom, by using one of his favourite words (*relentlessly*: 5: 20; 6: 5; 12: 9 'stern'; 18: 15), which is not found in the Septuagint, indicated that the judgement on rulers was inescapable. In contrast, *The small man may find pity and forgiveness.*

7–8. God is *obsequious to none*: i.e. subject only to himself and all are treated *equally* by him. Therefore forgiveness does not come to the poor to compensate for his low estate. *he reserves the sternest inquisition* for *the powerful* because to them greater stewardship was entrusted.

9–11. The writer exhorted man to *learn wisdom* which is still in this context understood as human know-how, gained by experience coupled with understanding of, and obedience to, God's will (*kept a holy course*), and so *not go astray.* ✱

Wisdom shines bright and never fades; she is easily dis- 12 cerned by those who love her, and by those who seek her she is found. She is quick to make herself known to those 13

14 who desire knowledge of her; the man who rises early in search of her will not grow weary in the quest, for he will
15 find her seated at his door. To set all one's thoughts on her is prudence in its perfect shape, and to lie wakeful in
16 her cause is the short way to peace of mind. For she herself ranges in search of those who are worthy of her; on their daily path she appears to them with kindly intent, and in
17 all their purposes meets them half-way. The true beginning of wisdom is the desire to learn, and a concern for learning
18 means love towards her; the love of her means the keeping of her laws; to keep her laws is a warrant of immortality;
19, 20 and immortality brings a man near to God. Thus the
21 desire of wisdom leads to kingly stature. If, therefore, you value your thrones and your sceptres, you rulers of the nations, you must honour wisdom, so that you may reign for ever.

✲ These verses contain the major statement on divine wisdom personified as God's agent. This idea is important in the development of a doctrine of grace. Man needs help in addition to his own natural capacity to reach his ultimate destiny. At the most basic level such help is needed to know how to search for God. And those who know God are successful (cp. 13: 1 – the fool who is condemned because he is ignorant of God). While man searches for God, God searches for man (Isa. 65: 1–2, 'I was there to be sought by a people who did not ask...I said, "Here am I, here am I"...I spread out my hands all day appealing to an unruly people').

12. *bright...easily discerned*: finding wisdom is not an impossible task. In 7: 25–6 wisdom's brightness is described as 'pure effluence' from God, a 'flawless mirror' of God's power. The expression *never fades* is often equated with immortality in Greek pagan writings.

13–16. Wisdom *meets them half-way*. These verses describe

46

the active searching for wisdom and her constant availability. Man rises early, has a single purpose (*set all one's thoughts on her*), and lies *wakeful* for her. At the same time wisdom is *seated at his door, ranges in search, appears to them*, and *meets them half-way*. The key to this mutual search is in the phrases *those who desire knowledge of her* and *those who are worthy of her* both in their outer life (*daily path*) and in their inner life (*their purposes*). The *worthy* are best explained as contrasting with the ungodly, who are unworthy because they court death (1: 16 'fit members of [death's] party'; 2: 24 'the experience of [death] is reserved for those who take his side') and do not care whether any trace of their life is left (2: 9; 5: 7, 13).

17–21. Having argued that man should learn wisdom, the author now considered how he should begin this acquisition. The reasoning in these verses follows a literary form often used in Greek philosophy. The statements are closely reasoned, in such a way that the conclusion of each statement becomes the premise of the next until the main conclusion is reached (verse 20). The desire for wisdom is understood since it is the theme of verses 12–16. Therefore since each subject is the previous predicate the reasoning runs: the desire for wisdom is the beginning of wisdom; the true beginning of wisdom is the desire to learn; etc. The conclusion of all is 'thus the desire of wisdom leads to kingly stature', which is the goal intended for everyman in this life. Verse 21 with its key-word 'therefore' is parallel to the argument in verses 17–20, while at the same time introducing the conclusion of a lengthy discussion which began at 1: 1. The whole section reads: 'Love justice, you rulers of the earth...' (1: 1); 'Hear, then, you kings...' (6: 1); 'If...you value your thrones...you must honour wisdom' (6: 21).

17. *The true beginning of wisdom is the desire to learn, and a concern for learning*: in the Old Testament the beginning of wisdom is the fear of God (Prov. 1: 7). This exhortation to active good is best understood in contrast to the way of the ungodly who neither desire God nor obey his laws.

18. *warrant of immortality*: furthers the contrast because the Greek idea behind *immortality* is 'incorruption'. The author of Wisdom adopted the Greek philosophical term to express the innate quality of man's nature. Hence in 2: 23 we read that God created man for incorruption while death came through corruption (2: 24).

19. *near to God*: means likeness ('the image of his own eternal self' 2: 23), rather than proximity. Incorruption brings man *near to God* through 'kinship with wisdom' (8: 17), which avoids evil (1: 4), and through knowledge of God's power (15: 3). Again, the wicked cannot be near God because they are corrupt.

20. *kingly stature*: man, created in God's likeness, is destined to rule. Also 2 Tim. 2: 12 states 'we shall reign with him'. ✶

A LINK PASSAGE

22 What wisdom is, and how she came into being, I will tell you; I will hide no secret from you. From her first beginnings I will trace out her course, and bring the knowledge of her into the light of day; I will not leave the truth 23 untold. Pale envy shall not travel in my company, for the 24 spiteful man will have no share in wisdom. Wise men in plenty are the world's salvation, and a prudent king is the 25 sheet-anchor of his people. Learn what I have to teach you, therefore, and it will be for your good.

✶ 'What wisdom is' is discussed in 7: 22ff. while 'how she came into being' is not treated here but is well known from Prov. 8: 24–31 and Job 28: 20–8. Since the author did not fulfil his own intention he may have intended 6: 22 – 9: 18 to describe the effect that wisdom had on Solomon. Furthermore, these verses hint at a number of ideas to be more fully developed in chs. 7: 1–11: 1: 'no secret' (7: 17–27); 'her

first beginnings' (10: 1 – 11: 1); 'knowledge of her' (7: 17);
'no share' (8: 18); 'the world's salvation' (9: 18); 'a prudent
king' (7: 7, 16; 8: 6–7, 18, 21).

25. *Learn*: be instructed, which is the key idea in this section
of the book (6: 17). ✳

THE LIFE OF THE KING (SOLOMON)

✳ In these chapters (7–9) the pursuit of wisdom is discussed
in the first person as if the king were speaking (see especially
7: 1–3, 7–10; 8: 2, 9–12; 9: 5, 11–12). Chs. 7–8 deal with
the nature and philosophy of the king who seeks to be a Godfearing ruler. Ch. 9 is couched in prayer-form.   ✳

THE KING (SOLOMON) IS ONLY A MAN

I too am a mortal man like all the rest, descended from **7**
the first man, who was made of dust, and in my mother's 2
womb I was wrought into flesh during a ten-months space,
compacted in blood from the seed of her husband and the
pleasure that is joined with sleep. When I was born, 3
I breathed the common air and was laid on the earth that
all men tread; and the first sound I uttered, as all do, was
a cry; they wrapped me up and nursed me and cared for 4
me. No king begins life in any other way; for all come 5, 6
into life by a single path, and by a single path go out again.

Therefore I prayed, and prudence was given to me; 7
I called for help, and there came to me a spirit of wisdom.
I valued her above sceptre and throne, and reckoned 8
riches as nothing beside her; I counted no precious stone 9
her equal, because all the gold in the world compared
with her is but a little sand, and silver worth no more than
clay. I loved her more than health and beauty; I preferred 10

11 her to the light of day; for her radiance is unsleeping. So all good things together came to me with her, and in her
12 hands was wealth past counting; and all was mine to enjoy, for all follows where wisdom leads, and I was in
13 ignorance before, that she is the beginning of it all. What I learnt with pure intention I now share without grudging, nor do I hoard for myself the wealth that comes from her.
14 She is an inexhaustible treasure for mankind, and those who profit by it become God's friends, commended to him by the gifts they derive from her instruction.

✶ Even the noble ruler is mortal like every other man; an opinion held also by the ungodly (2: 1–9). However, the conclusion in the two sections is totally different. To the ungodly, all material things are to be enjoyed to the full, for the end is death and no trace is left. Beginning from the same premise of man's mortality, the author maintained that whoever pursues wisdom receives everything and lives forever. The logic of the argument is that since the king is mortal (7: 1–6) *therefore* (7: 7–14) he needs God.

1–2. The emphasis is on the body; a purely Hebraic idea. The writer's emphasis on the mortality of the king may be so as to challenge the tendency in the hellenistic world to deify a ruler. The suggestion that the king is mortal supports our basic thesis that the writer was really describing everyman. At no point did the writer identify the king as Solomon (see pp. 1–2).

descended from the first man: from Adam (*first man* is a new noun-formation by the author) who was made from earth. *flesh* merely means that he is mortal and is not to be contrasted with spirit (cp. 15: 8, 11). *mother's womb*...*ten-months* again suggests mortality; ...*blood*...*seed* reflects the contemporary view of how the embryo is formed.

7. With this verse we begin to understand to what extent the author thought of Solomon as the prototype of man.

prayed: cp. 8: 21 which introduces the prayer recorded in
ch. 9. *prudence...spirit of wisdom* are gifts granted through
prayer. To the author they are synonyms.

8–10. The idea of wisdom being incomparable is expressed
often in the Old Testament. Wealth, health, beauty are not to
be preferred to wisdom. To the ungodly (2: 7–9) these qualities were everything. Wisdom is *unsleeping*, hence better than
the light of day (cp. 7: 29).

11–14. The phrase *all good things* is explained by the parallel
wealth past counting. The king had no ulterior motive, since he
was *in ignorance before* finding wisdom *that she is the beginning
of it all*, and *learnt with pure intention*. He was a perfect steward
of all that came to him as a result of finding wisdom: *share
without grudging, nor do I hoard, treasure for mankind*. And the
final result is that those who profit from wisdom become
God's friends. ✳

THE KING GAINS KNOWLEDGE THROUGH WISDOM

God grant that I may speak according to his will, and 15
that my own thoughts may be worthy of his gifts; for
even wisdom is under God's direction and he corrects the
wise; we and our words, prudence and knowledge and 16
craftsmanship, all are in his hand. He himself gave me true 17
understanding of things as they are: a knowledge of the
structure of the world and the operation of the elements;
the beginning and end of epochs and their middle course; 18
the alternating solstices and changing seasons; the cycles 19
of the years and the constellations; the nature of living 20
creatures and behaviour of wild beasts; the violent force
of winds and the thoughts of men; the varieties of plants
and the virtues of roots. I learnt it all, hidden or manifest, 21
for I was taught by her whose skill made all things, 22*a*
wisdom.

✳ 15–16. An appeal for divine inspiration. Such phrases as *according to his will* and *we and our words, prudence and knowledge and craftsmanship, are all in his hand* reflect Exod. 4: 11 which asks rhetorically: 'Who is it that gives man speech?' All we possess comes from God (cp. Eccles. 9: 1 'the righteous and the wise and all their doings are under God's control').

17–22. These verses contain a careful integration of Greek and Hebrew thought utilized to demonstrate the king's encyclopaedic knowledge obtained through associating with wisdom. It is no superficial synthesis but a valid demonstration of how the writer valued the Greek humanistic learning and culture in which he was educated and how he considered it to have contributed to the total revelation of God's uniqueness. His readers would understand the current literary and philosophical language of Alexandria and so the writer's message would be completely relevant.

17–20. *true understanding of things as they are* introduces the spheres where God reveals himself: (1) *the structure of the world*: i.e. the construction of the physical world; (2) *the operation of the elements*: earth, air, fire, and water (cp. 13: 2; 19: 18); (3) *the beginning and end of epochs and their middle course*: the chronology of world history rather than the change of seasons; (4) *the alternating solstices*: astronomy; (5) *the cycles of the years*: lunar and solar systems and the harmonizing of the two, because the Jews followed a lunar calendar; (6) *the constellations*: astrology; (7) *the nature of living creatures and behaviour of wild beasts*: zoology (cp. 16: 5); (8) *the violent force of winds*: the demons to whom both the Jews and pagans assigned powerful influence in the world. It was necessary to know the attributes of each in order to control them; (9) *the thoughts of men*: psychology; (10) *the varieties of plants and the virtues of roots*: botany and pharmacy.

21–2 a. *I learnt it all* sums up the discussion so far. *hidden or manifest* means 'everything', not just the two categories stated: Hebrew often uses such word-pairs in this broad sense, e.g. 'high and low', 'good and evil'. Wisdom is described as the

one *whose skill made all things*. Wisdom was with God when
he created the world (Prov. 8: 22, 'The LORD created me the
beginning of his works'). In 9: 1–2 wisdom is the agent of
God's creative will while in 8: 6 and 14: 2 (in some witnesses)
she is the active cause of all. In 13: 1 God is the craftsman.
These different ways of describing wisdom are not to be taken
as mutually exclusive of each other but as complementary. ✳

WISDOM'S ATTRIBUTES

For in wisdom there is a spirit intelligent and holy, 22*l*
unique in its kind yet made up of many parts, subtle,
free-moving, lucid, spotless, clear, invulnerable,[a] loving
what is good, eager, unhindered, beneficent, kindly to- 23
wards men, steadfast, unerring, untouched by care, all-
powerful, all-surveying, and permeating all intelligent,
pure, and delicate spirits. For wisdom moves more easily 24
than motion itself, she pervades and permeates all things
because she is so pure. Like a fine mist she rises from the 25
power of God, a pure effluence from the glory of the
Almighty; so nothing defiled can enter into her by stealth.
She is the brightness that streams from[b] everlasting light, 26
the flawless mirror of the active power of God and the
image of his goodness. She is but one, yet can do every- 27
thing; herself unchanging, she makes all things new; age
after age she enters into holy souls and makes them God's
friends and prophets, for nothing is acceptable to God but 28
the man who makes his home with wisdom. She is more 29
radiant than the sun, and surpasses every constellation;
compared with the light of day, she is found to excel; for 30

[a] invulnerable: *or* working no harm.
[b] *Or* She is the reflection of...

day gives place to night, but against wisdom no evil can
8 prevail. She spans the world in power from end to end,
and orders all things benignly.

✳ Twenty-one attributes, although the total varies in other
versions, represents a multiple of the magical number seven.
Such use of seven and three are equally common in Greek and
Jewish writings. Even though twenty-one qualities are assigned
to wisdom her true nature remains elusive. There is no particular order to the listing and some attributes are repeated in
order to achieve the desired total. Philo referred to wisdom as
'many-named'. The main characteristics are basic to the
author's overall view of wisdom. It is important to emphasize
that although wisdom is strongly personified, nowhere is she
portrayed as an entity independent of God. Although in Greek
philosophical writing many of these attributes were assigned
to the idea of 'word' (*logos*), the author has chosen wisdom
to emphasize the biblical orientation, where wisdom was one
of the main avenues for divine revelation after the conclusion
of the prophetic movement. No doctrine of the personification
of 'word' (*logos*) developed in the Old Testament.

22*b*–24. Wisdom's qualities: *in wisdom there is a spirit*: i.e.
wisdom's essential life principle. In other passages the spirit of
the Lord is said to be all-encompassing (cp. 1: 7; 12: 1). Also
wisdom's spirit is *holy* (cp. 9: 17) but it is not the third member
of the Trinity; *unique in its kind yet made up of many parts*:
i.e. unity within a diversity of manifestations and, of course,
single in kind; *subtle*: thin, fine (used of the manna in Exod.
16: 14ff.); *free-moving*: cp. verse 24 where she penetrates
everything because she is pure; *lucid*: cp. 10: 21 – in the Old
Testament God made man's mouth to speak; *spotless*: in spite
of its contacts with the world; *clear*: distinct; *invulnerable*:
unable to suffer injury as the Old Testament says that God
cannot be injured; *loving what is good*: cp. 1: 6 and 12: 19 – the
closest in English is 'philanthropic' – also note the subsequent

attribute *kindly towards men* which is a synonym; *all-powerful*: cp. 11: 17 and 18: 15; *all-surveying*: cp. 1: 7–8 ('the spirit of the Lord') and 1: 9–10 (God himself); *permeating all...spirits* which are intelligent, pure and subtle; *spirits* in the broadest sense of angels and human-beings. Wisdom enters into those spirits who have an affinity with her.

25–6. Wisdom's derivation. The emphasis is on *power of God, glory of the Almighty, everlasting light, active power of God,* and *his goodness* as the source of wisdom, rather than on the form wisdom takes as expressed in such words as *effluence, brightness, flawless mirror,* and *image.* Wisdom is not indepen-dent but derives her identity from God. Hence, she is personi-fied as *a fine mist* rising as the power of God. Words such as *streams from, mirror, image* underline the fact that wisdom is a reflection of God and not the source of her own identity. The Greek behind *streams from* can denote either the light emitted from a luminary or the reflection. Here it is the latter.

7: 27 – 8: 1. The activity of wisdom in the world: many of the statements in this section have already appeared in verses 22ff.

27. *God's friends and prophets,* although *friends* is a term not found in the Septuagint, it is certainly a familiar idea in this book (cp. 7: 14). Philo stated that all wise men were 'friends of God'. The basis for this friendship is his love for all his creation (11: 24; 13: 4–5). Jesus called his disciples 'friends' (John 15: 14–15).

28. *makes his home* is marriage terminology (cp. 8: 2; 9: 10); compare our expression 'wedded to his books'.

29. *constellation...light* etc.: the simile is in the same vein as verses 25–6.

8: 1. Belongs with the preceding and concludes the thought. Wisdom is all-encompassing and *orders,* i.e. governs. Although the term is used in Greek household management and was popular with some Greek philosophers, the idea of the divine government of the world is biblical. ✳

THE KING'S DESIRE FOR WISDOM AS HIS BRIDE

2 Wisdom I loved; I sought her out when I was young
and longed to win her for my bride, and I fell in love
3 with her beauty. She adds lustre to her noble birth,
because it is given her to live with God, and the Lord of
4 all things has accepted her. She is initiated into the knowledge that belongs to God, and she decides for him what
5 he shall do. If riches are a prize to be desired in life, what
6 is richer than wisdom, the active cause of all things? If
prudence shows itself in action, who more than wisdom
7 is the artificer of all that is? If virtue is the object of a man's
affections, the fruits of wisdom's labours are the virtues;
temperance and prudence, justice and fortitude, these are
her teaching, and in the life of men there is nothing of
8 more value than these. If a man longs, perhaps, for great
experience, she knows the past, she can infer what is to
come; she understands the subtleties of argument and the
solving of problems, she can read signs and portents, and
9 can foretell the outcome of events and periods. So I determined to bring her home to live with me, knowing that
she would be my counsellor in prosperity and my com-
10 fort in anxiety and grief. Through her, I thought, I shall
win fame in the eyes of the people and honour among
11 older men, young though I am. When I sit in judgement,
I shall prove myself acute, and the great men will admire
12 me; when I say nothing, they will wait for me to speak;
when I speak they will attend, and though I hold forth at
length, they will lay a finger to their lips and listen.
13 Through her I shall have immortality, and shall leave an
14 undying memory to those who come after me. I shall rule

over many peoples, and nations will become my subjects.
Grim tyrants will be frightened when they hear of me; 15
among my own people I shall show myself a good king,
and on the battlefield a brave one. When I come home, 16
I shall find rest with her; for there is no bitterness in her
company, no pain in life with her, only gladness and joy.

✻ 2. *I loved; I sought her. . .longed to win her for my bride, and
I fell in love with her beauty* suggests the intensity of the passion
the king had for wisdom. The Greek word for *loved* suggests
sexual love, which is not the usual biblical term to describe
man's love for God although it is used to describe God's love
for Christ (John 5: 20; 16: 27) and man's love for Christ
(1 Cor. 16: 22). Other writers also have described wisdom as
wife/mother.

3–4. *her noble birth* is because of her intimacy with God. The
Greek term for *live with God* may suggest a conjugal relationship, but in contemporary Greek prose it often meant only
companionship. The latter translation is preferable here, to
avoid any suggestion that wisdom was both God's wife and
man's bride. Also verse 4, portraying wisdom as God's craftsman, reflects the same idea (cp. 8: 9–10). In Prov. 8: 22–31,
wisdom is described as being created by God before he made
the world and sharing in the subsequent creative acts, which is
the idea here. Wisdom, the king's bride, leaves God, with
whom she gained nobility, and comes to ennoble her husband.

5–16. These verses describe the benefits of loving wisdom.
Verses 5–8 set forth four conditions of life which, if desired,
are obtained through wisdom, and will produce certain results
described in verses 9–16. The conditions of life are: (1) *riches*:
cp. 'In my hands are riches. . .boundless wealth' (Prov. 8: 18);
(2) *prudence*: in the technical sense of practical wisdom (cp.
3: 15; 4: 9; 6: 15; 7: 7, 16; 8: 7, 18, 21). Even in the practical
realm only wisdom can actually fashion things; (3) *virtue*
(verse 7): in the N.E.B. this is an unfortunate translation;

better 'justice' (the same Greek word as in 1: 1). In this verse wisdom is the progenitor of the four virtues of Greek philosophy which are also the four cardinal virtues of Christianity. They were also current in Alexandria. The significant point to be noted is that these virtues are said to be the work of wisdom. They are *temperance*: i.e. self-control (the only time it is mentioned in this book); *prudence*: which is in the preceding verse; *justice*: cp. 12: 16; 14: 7 (N.E.B. 'right'); 9: 3; 15: 3 (N.E.B. 'righteousness'); and *fortitude*: i.e. courage (8: 15); (4) *great experience*: knowledge based on past experience: wisdom's ability to read the past correctly in order to anticipate the future. The practical bent of wisdom's capacity is shown in *subtleties of argument* and *solving of problems* as well as foretelling *the outcome of events and periods*, which means the unfolding of history rather than the matter of seasonal changes. We note that these functions are typically Hebraic and contrast with the Greek ideas of the preceding verse in order to emphasize the wide range of wisdom's power.

9–16. The results of those conditions of life obtained through wisdom are introduced by 'So'. 'knowing that' indicates the king's astute evaluation of wisdom's advantage to him, so that he 'determined' to have her as his bride in order to be sure of receiving those attributes so highly esteemed in his day.

9–13. Depicts the king as a wise man. The marks of the wise man are good works he does in this life as was also the case for the barren woman and the eunuch (3: 13ff.): (1) *counsellor in prosperity*: cp. 7: 11; (2) *be...my comfort in anxiety*: 'speak softly' or 'comfort' – a quality not found in other passages; (3) *fame in the eyes of the people*: i.e. 'well known in the city gate' (Prov. 31: 23), where important decisions were taken; (4) *honour among older men*: while still young. Compare 9: 6; (5) *in judgement, I shall prove myself acute*: cp. 1 Kings 3: 16–28 for Solomon's brilliant judgement concerning the child claimed by two different women; (6) *great men will admire*: i.e. Hiram of Tyre (1 Kings 4: 34; 5: 1) and the queen of Sheba (1 Kings 10: 1–9); (7) *when*

I speak...they will lay a finger to their lips and listen: a sign of respect or of being dumbfounded; here it is the former; (8) the phrase *immortality, and shall leave an undying memory* contains synonymous ideas. Clearly in this verse *immortality* is achieved by *an undying memory* (cp. 4: 1), which is a re-statement of the old Jewish idea of being remembered for one's good deeds. We should note that in 8: 17 and 15: 3 close association with wisdom is immortality (cp. also 1: 15).

14–15. Depict the king as ruler of whom it is said: (1) he will *rule over many peoples*; through wisdom the ruler's influence will extend beyond national boundaries; (2) *Grim tyrants will be frightened* of him: according to 1 Kings 10: 23–5 'Solomon outdid all the kings of the earth in wealth and wisdom' and so they each sent gifts to him.

16. At home wisdom provides the king with *rest* (cp. 6: 15 'peace of mind') and companionship. *gladness and joy*, the opposite of *bitterness*, are emotions connected with wisdom in other passages and suggest the dwelling-place of virtuous souls. Also, wisdom provides 'pure delight' (verse 18).

It is interesting to note that the author of this book followed Chronicles in remaining silent about Solomon's deviations from the ideal life. It was the author's purpose to outline the perfect life not only for Solomon but for everyman, and hence such deviations were irrelevant. Note also that this view of life with wisdom is contrary to that expressed by Ecclesiastes, who saw life as a vexation which increased in proportion to the gain in knowledge. For Ecclesiastes there was no *gladness and joy*. ✳

THE KING DECIDES TO PRAY FOR THE GIFT OF WISDOM

I thought this over in my mind, and I perceived that in 17 kinship with wisdom lies immortality and in her friend- 18 ship is pure delight; that in doing her work is wealth that cannot fail, to be taught in her school gives understanding,

and an honourable name is won by converse with her. So
I went about in search of some way to win her for my
19 own. As a child I was born to excellence, and a noble soul
20 fell to my lot; or rather, I myself was noble, and I entered
21 into an unblemished body; but I saw that there was no
way to gain possession of her except by gift of God – and
it was a mark of understanding to know from whom that
gift must come. So I pleaded with the Lord, and from the
depths of my heart I prayed to him in these words.

✷ 17–18. *thought this over in my mind*: the king recapitulates
all wisdom's merits and decides to opt for her: (1) *immortality*
is found *in kinship with wisdom*; (2) *pure delight* is found *in
friendship* with her; (3) unfailing *wealth* is earned *in doing her
work*; (4) *understanding* is gained in her company, i.e. in the
mutual exchange between teacher and pupil; (5) *an honourable
name is won* by coming in contact with her.

19–20. The king states that he was *born to excellence* which
means that he has *a noble soul* and *an unblemished body*. We may
well ask why these verses on anthropology are introduced
into a section (verses 17–21) dealing with the benefits of seeking wisdom. Verses 19–20 are in parenthesis but essential to
the thesis expressed in this section. The possession of wisdom is
a gift to those who ask and is not dependent upon excellence
of birth ('So I went about in search' (verse 18)...'but I saw
that there was no way to gain possession of her except by
gift of God' (verse 21)).

These verses have precipitated much discussion, including
the suggestion by some scholars that a hint of the doctrine
of original sin is found here. Along with 1: 4, 9: 15 and 15:
8–13 they are the key passages for understanding Wisdom's
views on the nature of man. Already in 7: 1–6 the writer has
described the physical origins of man including even those
of the wise king. But man's purely human qualities are not

enough to guarantee his obtaining divine wisdom. This fact is made quite clear even in the arguments of the ungodly, who understood themselves to be born by 'mere chance' (2: 2). In isolation these verses might be understood as arguing for the pre-existence of the soul but the author never spoke of the soul as being older than the body. In the context of the whole book the writer was stressing the pre-eminence of the soul rather than its pre-existence.

These verses are another example of the author's ability to blend Greek and Hebrew thought. The question concerns the meaning of *soul* and *body*. The author at no time considered them as two independent substances. In Hebrew thought the tendency was to connect personality with the body while Greek philosophy favoured associating personality with the soul. The writer has taken a tentative step in the direction of Greek thinking while at the same time rejecting an either/or conclusion. The thought expressed in the words *body* and *soul* and in the phrase *entered into* is that of the integration of human personality in man as a totality.

The specific literary device of contrast expressed by *or rather* allowed the author to stress the significant: the pre-eminence of man's intellectual and moral powers (cp. 9: 15 where 'soul' is parallel to 'mind') rather than the fact of his physical existence. Such a literary device tends to lay the greater stress on the first part of the comparison (*noble soul*) without totally excluding the second part (*unblemished body*). In this instance the idea of an *unblemished body* is a new concept in a world dominated by Greek philosophy but common within the biblical context. The literary technique itself is biblical ('but now that you do acknowledge God – or rather, now that he has acknowledged you', Gal. 4: 9).

21. *a mark of understanding to know*: even when man has achieved the fullest expression of human perfection he still falls short of the divine design for man: immortality (cp. 2: 23). And so he must pray for divine wisdom (*I pleaded with the Lord...prayed to him*). *

PRAYER FOR THE GIFT OF WISDOM

9 God of our fathers, merciful Lord, who hast made all
2 things by thy word, and in thy wisdom hast fashioned
3 man, to be the master of thy whole creation, and to be
steward of the world in holiness and righteousness, and to
4 administer justice with an upright heart, give me wisdom,
who sits beside thy throne, and do not refuse me a place
5 among thy servants. I am thy slave, thy slave-girl's son,
a weak ephemeral man, too feeble to understand justice
6 and law; for let a man be ever so perfect in the eyes of his
fellow-men, if the wisdom that comes from thee is want-
7 ing, he will be of no account. Thou didst choose me to be
king of thy own people, and judge over thy sons and
8 daughters; thou didst tell me to build a temple on thy
sacred mountain and an altar in the city which is thy
dwelling-place, a copy of the sacred tabernacle prepared
9 by thee from the beginning. And with thee is wisdom,
who is familiar with thy works and was present at the
making of the world by thee, who knows what is accept-
10 able to thee and in line with thy commandments. Send
her forth from the holy heavens, and from thy glorious
throne bid her come down, so that she may labour at my
11 side and I may learn what pleases thee. For she knows and
understands all things, and will guide me prudently in all
12 I do, and guard me in her glory. So shall my life's work
be acceptable, and I shall judge thy people justly, and be
13 worthy of my father's throne. For how can any man learn
what is God's plan? How can he apprehend what the
14 Lord's will is? The reasoning of men is feeble, and our
15 plans are fallible; because a perishable body weighs down

the soul, and its frame of clay burdens the mind so full of
thoughts. With difficulty we guess even at things on earth, 16
and laboriously find out what lies before our feet; and who
has ever traced out what is in heaven? Who ever learnt 17
to know thy purposes, unless thou hadst given him wisdom and sent thy holy spirit down from heaven on high?
Thus it was that those on earth were set upon the right 18
path, and men were taught what pleases thee; thus were
they preserved by wisdom.

✻ No matter how perfect man becomes he is still in need of
God's gift of wisdom. Although this chapter is presented as
the king's prayer it is also everyman's prayer for divine grace.
The imagery shifts easily from referring to the king to being
applicable to everyman.

The prayer is composed of (1) elements drawn from the
historic prayer of Solomon (1 Kings 3: 6–9); (2) thoughts
common to wisdom literature; and (3) reflections of the
author himself, especially verses 13–18.

The chapter can be divided into (1) address to God (1–3;
7–9); (2) petition (4, 10–12); (3) motive and general observation (5–6, 13–18). Verse 18, which is the conclusion to the
prayer, also serves as the introduction to ch. 10.

1–3. Addresses the *God of our fathers* and so sets the prayer
within the mainstream of Jewish religion; *fathers*: the patriarchs. God is also *merciful* and a creator God. The latter idea is
expressed by *made* and *fashioned*. God expresses his creativity
in his *word* which is not the Greek *logos* but the creative word
of Gen. 1 ('and God said...') and of Ps. 33: 6 ('The LORD's
word made the heavens') and of Wisdom. Furthermore, God's
creative act results in man becoming *master of thy whole creation*
and *steward of the world*.

The phraseology is an excellent representation of Hebraic
literary style. By a series of parallels (*made/fashioned*; *master/
steward*) the writer built up a comprehensive picture, moving

from the concept of the creative God to that of man, his steward. Furthermore, the stewardship is spelled out as the administering of *justice with an upright heart*.

4–6. How can man fulfil his stewardship? *give me wisdom ...and do not refuse me a place among thy servants*: wisdom *sits beside* God's *throne* as assessor (verse 4) and associate (8: 4) and was with God at the making of the world (verse 9) and so is indispensable if the king's public life is to be successful.

In the light of 8: 18–21, the king (man), realizing himself to be *a weak ephemeral man* (verse 5), begs not to be rejected but to be counted *among thy servants*, that is, God's children. The term *slave* means home-born slave (Gen. 14: 14 'retainers, men born in his household') and consequently also means mortal. Furthermore, even if he is considered *perfect in the eyes of his fellow-men* he is inadequate without wisdom. These several terms are compounded to emphasize the inadequacy of man without God's grace, that is, wisdom.

7–9. These verses formulate the petition in terms of the need for the gift of wisdom so that the king can be *judge* (verse 7) and worshipper of God (builder of the *temple*, verse 8). The *sacred mountain* is Mount Moriah, which was already sacred in Abraham's time (Gen. 22: 2–4). The idea of the *dwelling-place* as a prototype *prepared by thee from the beginning* is also found in the New Testament and may well be based on a rabbinic story that certain things, including the temple, had existed before the foundation of the world.

10–12. Wisdom is sent forth from God's presence for certain specific purposes: (1) to *labour* at man's *side*; (2) to help man *learn what pleases* God; (3) to *guide* man *prudently*; (4) to *guard* man with her *glory*: wisdom emanates from God as power and goodness (7: 25–6). *So shall my life's work be acceptable*: the same argument as was found in 8: 5–16.

13–18. The questions *For how can any man learn what is God's plan?* and *How can he apprehend what the Lord's will is?* show that the author had everyman in mind when writing this prayer; not just the king. The Hebraic parallelism of thought

is found here in such phrases as *learn/apprehend, God's plan/
Lord's will*. The phraseology stems from Isa. 40: 13 where the
rhetorical question is whether anyone can comprehend God's
doings. Man's *reasoning* is *feeble* (verse 14), i.e. 'uncertain',
'wavering' if we look to Greek literature for the term, or
'cowardly' according to the New Testament understanding
of the word; and *fallible*, i.e. insecure (4: 4). The same idea is
re-stated in verse 16. Man's nature is that of *a perishable body*,
and its synonym *frame of clay*, wherein is the *soul/mind so full
of thoughts*. Here, the writer is using the same argument as in
8: 18–21. The statement about man's nature is an explanation,
not of sin, but of man's need for help. Consequently it is not
a description of the impurity of the body but of man's mortality. Man cannot rise above his limitations and so *know* God's
purpose without *wisdom* and its synonym the *holy spirit*
(verse 17).

Verse 18 sums up the prayer and introduces the historical
sketch in ch. 10. *those on earth* and its synonym *men* suggest
again the subject everyman. *preserved by wisdom* refers to
earthly well-being and not to eternal salvation. Although the
first appearance of *preserved*, which in the Greek means 'to
save', is in this verse, it becomes a basic theme in the following
section (10: 4; 14: 4–5; 16: 7, 11; 18: 5). In the first nine
chapters wisdom remained faithful to man until he found
salvation (was *preserved*). Now, in the second half of the book,
salvation becomes the key word; especially in the account of
the heroes of the sacred history. ✷

Divine wisdom in history

✷ Chs. 10–19 constitute the second part of the book. The
main theme is the beneficent action of wisdom in the history
of the children of Israel. The thesis is that the evil inflicted upon
the Egyptians or the Canaanites is a blessing to the Israelites.

This is the first attempt in Jewish literature to write a philosophy of history. The need for such a recital as proof of God's
faithfulness and ability to save was always necessary at times
of low morale. If God could deliver his people before from
such overwhelming oppression as was experienced in Egypt
he could do it again. In undertaking such a philosophy of
history the author was forced to take considerable licence in
the interpretation of the biblical text. Also in these chapters
much more extensive use is made of Jewish tradition as reflected in the targums than in chs. 1–9.

From an early period there were translations into Aramaic
(targums) which served to interpret the biblical text and make
it relevant to its hearers, We possess an official targum to the
Pentateuch (Onkelos) which, although originating in Palestine, was given final form in Babylonia and much later than
the time of Wisdom. At the same time we have still available
another targum tradition which was also Palestinian in origin
and remained so. For the Palestinian targums we possess two
slightly different texts: Pseudo-Jonathan and Neofiti 1. These
two targum texts are also late, in their present form, but contain valuable material originating from the earliest period of
rabbinic interpretation of the Bible (see *The Making of the Old
Testament*, pp. 154–6, for a fuller discussion of the targums).

Although there is no evidence that the author of Wisdom
knew or directly utilized these targums, reliance on such extra-
biblical sources as are reflected in the Palestinian targums may,
in part, explain the frequent divergence from the biblical text
proper. There are certainly a number of startling parallels
which will be noted. ✳

WISDOM AND GOD IN HISTORY

10 WISDOM IT WAS who kept guard over the first
father of the human race, when he alone had yet
2 been made; she saved him after his fall, and gave him the

strength to master all things. It was because a wicked man 3
forsook her in his anger that he murdered his brother in
a fit of rage, and so destroyed himself. Through his fault 4
the earth was covered with a deluge, and again wisdom
came to the rescue, and taught the one good man to pilot
his plain wooden hulk. It was she, when heathen nations 5
leagued in wickedness were thrown into confusion, who
picked out one good man and kept him blameless in the
sight of God, giving him strength to resist his pity for his
child. She saved a good man from the destruction of the 6
godless, and he escaped the fire that came down on the
Five Cities, cities whose wickedness is still attested by 7
a smoking waste, by plants whose fruit can never ripen,
and a pillar of salt standing there as a memorial of an unbelieving soul. Wisdom they ignored, and they suffered 8
for it, losing the power to recognize what is good and
leaving by their lives a monument of folly, such that their
enormities can never be forgotten. But wisdom brought 9
her servants safely out of their troubles. It was she, when 10
a good man was a fugitive from his brother's anger, who
guided him on the straight path; she showed him that
God is king, and gave him knowledge of his holiness;[a] she
prospered his labours and made his toil productive. When 11
men in their rapacity tried to exploit him, she stood by
him and made him rich. She kept him safe from his 12
enemies, and preserved him from treacherous attacks; she
gave him victory after a hard struggle, and taught him
that godliness is the greatest power of all. It was she who 13
refused to desert a good man when he was sold as a slave;

[a] showed...holiness: *or* gave him a vision of God's realm, and knowledge of his holy angels.

she preserved him from sin and went down into the
14 dungeon with him, nor did she leave him when he was in
chains until she had brought him sceptre and kingdom and
authority over his persecutors; she gave the lie to his
15 accusers, and brought him undying fame. It was she who
rescued a godfearing people, a blameless race, from a
16 nation of oppressors; she inspired a servant of the Lord,
and with his signs and wonders he defied formidable
17 kings. She rewarded the labours of godfearing men, she
guided them on a marvellous journey and became a
covering for them by day and a blaze of stars by night.
18 She brought them over the Red Sea and guided them
19 through its deep waters; but their enemies she engulfed,
20 and cast them up again out of the fathomless deep. So
good men plundered the ungodly; they sang the glories
of thy holy name, O Lord, and praised with one accord
21 thy power, their champion; for wisdom taught the dumb
to speak, and made the tongues of infants eloquent.

* The chapter is clearly divided into six sections by the
association of 'she', i.e. 'wisdom' (supplied by the N.E.B.
in 10: 1), and 'one good man'. Furthermore, verses 1–7 deal
with those rare good men who survived in a wicked world.
The word 'wisdom' in verses 8–9, which deal with the
Sodomites, suggest a unit marked off from what precedes and
follows. In verses 10–21 the description of the individual good
man is resumed.

The recitation of the highlights of Israel's history by the
events connected with typical individuals was usual in the Old
Testament (cp. Ps. 105). The same pattern persisted in the New
Testament (cp. Acts 7: 2–53; Heb. 11). The lists in Ps. 105,
Acts 7, and Heb. 11 all deal with those who through obedience
to God have furthered Israel's cause. The list of types reads

like a *Who's who* in the history of Israel. The same is true in
Wisdom except that the types are not identified by name.
This anonymity is significant (cp. 4: 10 on Enoch). In this
book the author wished to present a more comprehensive
view of man. In keeping with his practice of contrasting just
and ungodly men he includes Cain. Enoch, although usually
included in such lists, is not mentioned, probably because he
is already cited in 4: 10ff.

1–7. These verses deal with Adam, Noah, and Abraham.

1–2. *Wisdom*: the N.E.B. has supplied this for the 'she' of
the Greek text (cp. verses 5, 6, 10, 13, 15). The actual word only
appears twice in this chapter (verses 8–9) and only in two
additional places (14: 2, 5) in the whole second part of the
book. She is the active principle of good, leading, saving,
protecting men, and forsaken at their own peril. The idea that
wisdom guarded Adam (*the first father*) both before and after
the Fall is non-biblical but is the general view of Jewish and
Christian writers. *kept guard. . .when he alone had yet been made*:
there are three possible interpretations of *alone*: (1) Adam only
is created and all the rest are begotten; (2) Adam was un-
protected; (3) Adam was unique and there were no others to
detract from him. When we examine the Palestinian targum
tradition to Gen. 3: 22 for the phrase 'The man has become like
one of us' we find the third interpretation of *alone*. There are
three inter-related targumic versions and that in Neofiti 1
reflects the Wisdom text: 'And God said, "Behold the first
man whom I have made is unique in the world as I am unique
in the heavens above."' We may conclude that the uniqueness
of Adam is the correct interpretation because when the whole
future of the human race rested on him after the expulsion
wisdom *saved him* and *gave him the strength*. Even after the Fall
he is commissioned *to master all things*.

3. *a wicked man* (the opposite to 'a good man'): Cain, who
rejected wisdom *and so destroyed himself*. Consider 1: 15, which
states that righteousness is immortality. Hence here we are not
concerned with who destroyed Cain but with the fact that by

acting in an unrighteous manner Cain joined the 'devil's party' and so courted death.

4. *Through his fault...a deluge*: if *his* means Cain then the explanation is novel since in Gen. 6: 1ff. the flood was caused by the folly of the sons of God marrying the daughters of men and by the increasing wickedness upon earth. The *his* may well refer to Cain's descendants as some rabbis understood the Genesis text. Probably, in keeping with the writer's emphasis on everyman, *his* refers to the wicked in general. *one good man to pilot his plain wooden hulk*: Noah is the man and in 14: 6 he is 'the hope of mankind'. *good man* is the term the author always uses when referring to the Hebrew people. By contrast in 10: 6ff., the Sodomites are called 'godless'. *plain* emphasizes the inadequacy of the means for the important end just as in 14: 5 'frailest spar' and 'mere raft' are not derogatory.

5. *heathen nations leagued in wickedness were thrown into confusion* reflects the concerted action to build the tower of Babel (Gen. 11: 7–9). *picked out*: 'knew' in the sense of 'respected'. And so wisdom loved Abraham. *to resist his pity for his child* refers to the sacrifice of Isaac in Gen. 22. The targum reflects the same idea when it writes: '(Abraham) does not falter'.

6–7. Lot is also *a good man*. The biblical reference is to Gen. 19: 17ff. but *fire that came down* is vocabulary unique to this book. The *Five Cities* are Sodom, Gomorrah, Admah, Zeboim, and Zoar/Bela. In Gen. 14: 2 only Zoar is spared so that Lot could flee thither. However, Josephus recorded a tradition that all five cities were destroyed. *still attested by a smoking waste*: Philo says it was still smoking in his day. The *pillar of salt...as a memorial of an unbelieving soul* refers to Lot's wife, who came from Sodom and who found the whole cataclysm unbelievable.

8–9. Contains a general observation about the contrast between wicked and good men. Verse 8 does not refer exclusively to Sodom but records the penalty paid for ignoring God and wisdom: the wicked became spiritually blind and also became a monument to the folly of mankind. In contrast, verse 9 states the benefit to good men.

10–21. These verses resume the sketch of saving history based on specific typical individuals (Jacob, Joseph, and Moses).

10–12. 'brought her servants safely out of their troubles', in verse 9, expresses the thesis that out of adversity comes salvation. The events in Jacob's life demonstrating the thesis are: (1) he *was a fugitive from his brother's anger*; (2) *men in their rapacity tried to exploit him* (Laban); (3) he was in danger of *treacherous attacks* (from Esau); (4) he gained the *victory after a hard struggle*: the struggle with the angel at Peniel. Out of all this God set Jacob on *the straight path* and *taught him that god-liness is the greatest power of all*.

13–14. *a good man...sold as a slave*: Joseph. Wisdom again acted as a protector and *preserved him from sin*: i.e. the tempt-ation of Potiphar's wife.

15. Israel is described here as a *godfearing people* and *a blame-less race*. By using such terminology the writer has dismissed from his account those occasions of infidelity of which the children of Israel had been guilty in the wilderness. This positive emphasis is correct since the writer was stressing the fact that Israel is God's people.

16. *she inspired a servant of the Lord*: Moses. In the Old Testament Moses is often called 'servant' while, in this con-text, the writer of Wisdom also gave the title to Aaron (18:21). Wisdom inspired him to defy *formidable kings*: plural in the text but actually only one king, Pharaoh.

17–19. Through Moses, wisdom supported Israel in a num-ber of ways: (1) *rewarded the labours of godfearing men*: that is, the ideal Israel represented by Moses. On the other hand, the Israelites fleeing Egypt did not leave empty-handed; (2) *guided them on a marvellous journey*: this refers to the water from the rock, the manna, and the quail. The writer interpreted the phrase 'the LORD went before them' (Exod. 13:21) as referring to wisdom, which he identified with the cloud. Here the cloud

71

is interpreted as a *covering*, as in the targum, more than a guide. Also, wisdom is called *a blaze of stars by night*, a unique description of 'a glowing fire' (Ps. 78: 14); (3) *their enemies she engulfed, and cast them up again out of the fathomless deep*: that is, the corpses of the Egyptians, who had been drowned, as in the Palestinian targum to Exod. 15: 12: 'The sea and the earth had a controversy one with the other. The sea said to the earth "receive thy children" and the earth said to the sea "receive thy murderers." But the earth willed not...and the sea willed not.'

20–1. Furthermore (*So*), when Israel saw the corpses they *plundered the ungodly*. The biblical account (Exod. 14: 30) does not state this but only that the Israelites saw the Egyptians 'lying dead on the sea-shore'. Josephus, however, recorded such a theft.

Then the Israelites *sang the glories*. Here the writer seems to be following the biblical order (Exod. 15: 1–21). *praised with one accord thy power* (God's): Philo wrote that Moses divided the people into two bands of men and women to sing in harmony to the creator. *wisdom taught the dumb to speak, and made the tongues of infants eloquent*: most of the commentators have failed to come to terms with this phrase in verse 21. For *dumb to speak* the writer has drawn on Isa. 35: 6 'and the tongue of the dumb shout aloud'. *the tongues of infants eloquent* also presents problems. Some scholars interpret this as meaning that wisdom loosened the tongues of the Israelites, who were otherwise unable to be eloquent in the name of God. The key to the interpretation may be found in the Palestinian targum to Exod. 15: 2 supported by a number of other rabbinic writings. The targum linked the experience of the Red Sea with the praise to God by the children by quoting texts drawn from other parts of the Old Testament: 'Our power and our praise, the indomitable of all ages, he is Yahweh. He speaks his word and he has been our Saviour. From the breast of their mother (Ps. 8: 2), the nurslings point at their fathers with their fingers and say: "he is our God who has nursed us on honey issuing from the rock (Deut. 32: 13) and with oil which issues from the heart of the rock. In the time when our mothers went out in the way and gave birth to us and left us there he sent an angel who washed us and oiled us (Ezek. 16: 4ff.). And now we will praise him...and we will sing his glory.'''

If the writer was indeed familiar with the targumic tradition, he has added a new dimension by treating the phrases *sang the glories/praised* and *dumb/tongues of infants* as synonyms. Consequently, th escope of the praises sung to God is extended. ✻

GOD'S FIDELITY TO HIS PEOPLE DEMONSTRATED BY THE EXODUS EXPERIENCE

✻ The basic theme of the book, the way of the just and the way of the ungodly, i.e. immortality and death, is further developed in chs. 11–19 by a series of proofs drawn from the history of Israel's sojourn in Egypt. Although 'wisdom' is mentioned in 11: 1 (and 14: 2, 5) the subject of these chapters is God (11: 4 'thee').

The literary form chosen by the writer for this part of the book was called 'measure for measure' by the Jewish rabbis. However, it is not unique to Jewish literature for it was probably borrowed initially from hellenistic histories where it was known as 'contrast'. This form has three aspects in these chapters. In 11: 5 that which is an instrument of vengeance for Egypt becomes a blessing for Israel. In 11: 16 that by which a man sins will also punish him. In 11: 9 the Israelites were also 'put to the test' so that they would understand how the Egyptians suffered. Six topics, drawn from the period of the wanderings in the wilderness, are discussed in a series of 'contrasts' to illustrate the idea of 'measure for measure': water (11: 5ff.), animals (11: 15ff.; 16: 1ff.), elements (fire, 16: 15ff.), light and darkness (17: 1 – 18: 4), death (18: 5ff.), and the Red Sea (19: 1ff.). Only the first of the 'contrasts' is discussed at this point, before the digression on idolatry in chs. 13–15.

The deliberate effort to organize the historical material in a series of striking 'contrasts' has required some modification of biblical details. The author has succeeded in creating a brilliant literary unit which is not a biblical commentary (*midrash*) in the strictest sense. He was able to formulate scripture selectively according to a specific Greek literary form, thus making the Bible more meaningful in contemporary life. The whole, therefore, has become a forceful defence of the idea of God's providence. ✳

WISDOM PRESERVED ISRAEL IN THE WANDERINGS

11 Wisdom, working through a holy prophet, brought
2 them success in all they did. They made their way across an unpeopled desert and pitched camp in untrodden wastes;
3 they resisted every enemy, and beat off hostile assaults.
4 When they were thirsty they called upon thee, and water to slake their thirst was given them out of the hard stone of a rocky cliff.

✳ 1–4. *a holy prophet* is Moses, who is singled out also in Deuteronomy and Hosea as the prophet who led Israel from Egypt. The path lay through the literally *unpeopled desert*. In their wanderings they were confronted by enemies and *hostile assaults*. The *enemy* were the Amalekites (Exod. 17: 8–16), the Canaanites of the Negeb (Num. 21: 1–3), the Amorites (Num. 21: 21–35), the Midianites (Num. 31: 1–12), Og of Bashan (Num. 21: 33–5). These verses reflect another time (cp. 10: 15 'blameless race') when the author's patriotic bias got the better of his judgement and he omitted all mention of the people's murmurings (Exod. 17: 3–6; Num. 20: 2–11) and instead mentioned only God's mercy in supplying their needs. The idea is to suggest that when the people's needs were great they naturally called upon the Lord. *called upon thee: thee* is not wisdom but God, who is the real subject of these chapters.

God is referred to as 'breath' (11: 20; 12: 1), 'word' (12: 9; 16: 12; 18: 15), 'hand' (11: 17; 14: 6; 16: 15; 19: 8), 'arm' (11: 21; 16: 16). ✶

THE FIRST 'CONTRAST' BETWEEN EGYPT AND ISRAEL: WATER

The self-same means by which their oppressors had been 5 punished were used to help them in their hour of need: those others found their river no unfailing stream of 6 water, but putrid and befouled with blood, in punish- 7 ment for their order that all the infants should be killed, while to these thou gavest abundant water unex- pectedly. So from the thirst they then endured, they 8 learnt how thou hadst punished their enemies; when 9 they themselves were put to the test, though discipline was tempered with mercy, they understood the tortures of the godless who were sentenced in anger. Thy own 10 people thou didst subject to an ordeal, warning them like a father; those others thou didst put to the torture, like a stern king passing sentence. At home and abroad, they 11 were equally in distress, for a double misery had come 12 upon them, and they groaned as they recalled the past. When they heard that the means of their own punishment 13 had been used to benefit thy people, they saw thy hand in it, O Lord. The man who long ago had been abandoned 14 and exposed, whom they had rejected with contumely, became in the event the object of their wonder and admiration; their thirst was such as the godly never knew.

✶ In these verses water is destruction to Egypt but salvation to Israel.

5–7. The key to these verses is the thirst of the Israelites quenched by *abundant water unexpectedly*, that is, the water from the rock in the wilderness (Num. 20: 11 'Water gushed out in abundance'). This contrasts with the Nile, *putrid and befouled with blood* (Exod. 7: 21, 24) and so with the unquenchable thirst of the Egyptians. (This is not a reference to the Egyptians drowning in the Red Sea.) The purpose of combining these two biblical passages from Exodus and Numbers was to show (1) the contrast of discipline: Egypt 'sentenced in anger' and Israel's discipline 'tempered with mercy' (verse 9); (2) the Egyptians' realization that this was God's doing: 'they saw thy hand in it' (verse 13). The author's method of exegesis was (1) to work from the known to the unknown: 'from the thirst they then endured, they learnt how thou hadst punished their enemies' (verse 8); (2) to assume that if Israel suffered how much more Egypt: 'when they themselves were put to the test,...they understood the tortures of the godless' (verse 9), i.e. the Egyptians.

11–12. *At home*, in the plagues, and *abroad*, in the Red Sea, the Egyptians suffered *a double misery*, for the water was their punishment and it was inflicted by God, not their own gods.

13. *the means of their own punishment had been used to benefit thy people* expresses the contrast of verse 5 in a variant form.

14. *The man...abandoned and exposed...became in the event the object of their wonder and admiration*: Moses, who was as an infant *abandoned and exposed* in the Nile; and then was *rejected with contumely*: the Egyptians' mocking rejection of Moses, which is an idea of the author's own fancy and not stated biblically. The phrase cannot refer to the Hebrews' doubts about Moses' God-given mission (Exod. 5: 21 'May this bring the LORD's judgement down upon you: you have made us stink in the nostrils of Pharaoh'). The author contrasted this *rejected* and despised Moses with Moses *the object of their wonder and admiration* as a 'holy prophet', at the end of *the event*, i.e. the triumphant exodus. *their thirst was such as the godly never knew*: the Egyptians suffered far more than the

Israelites even at their worst moment in the wanderings. This last phrase underlines the contrast between the *godly* and the *ungodly* in terms of thirst. ✳

PUNISHMENT FOR THE WORSHIP OF ANIMALS

In return for the insensate imagination of those wicked 15 men, which deluded them into worshipping reptiles devoid of reason, and mere vermin, thou didst send upon them a swarm of creatures devoid of reason to chastise them, and to teach them that the instruments of a man's 16 sin are the instruments of his punishment. For thy al- 17 mighty hand, which created the world out of formless matter, was not without other resource: it could have let loose upon them a host of bears or ravening lions or un- 18 known ferocious monsters newly created, either breathing out blasts of fire, or roaring and belching smoke, or flashing terrible sparks like lightning from their eyes, with 19 power not only to exterminate them by the wounds they inflicted, but by their mere appearance to kill them with fright. Even without these, a single breath would have 20 sufficed to lay them low, with justice in pursuit and the breath of thy power to blow them away; but thou hast ordered all things by measure and number and weight.

Great strength is thine to exert at any moment, and the 21 power of thy arm no man can resist, for in thy sight the 22 whole world is like a grain that just tips the scale or a drop of dew alighting on the ground at dawn. But thou art 23 merciful to all men because thou canst do all things; thou dost overlook the sins of men to bring them to repentance; for all existing things are dear to thee and thou hatest 24

nothing that thou hast created – why else wouldst thou
25 have made it? How could anything have continued in
existence, had it not been thy will? How could it have
26 endured unless called into being by thee? Thou sparest
all things because they are thine, our lord and master who
12 lovest all that lives; for thy imperishable breath is in them
all.

✳ In these verses and their contrast (15: 18 – 16: 14) concerning the worship of animals the writer is developing the
theme of Ps. 62: 11–12 '"Power belongs to God" and "True
love...is thine"; thou dost requite a man for his deeds.'

15–16. *the insensate imagination of those wicked men, which
deluded them*: according to Paul those who worship idols are
'misguided minds' and 'fools' (Rom. 1: 21–3). The punishment fits the crime, or, as a man sows so he reaps, is the argument advanced in verse 16. This discussion is re-opened in
15: 18 – 16: 14 where the Israelites are tested by the fiery
serpents and blessed by the quail in contrast to the suffering of
the Egyptians.

17. The idea of the inevitability of retribution, which is
confined to this world, is based on the fact that God *created
the world out of formless matter*. The terminology seems to refer
to the Greek concept of the four elements of fire, earth, water
and air, and the vocabulary belongs to that of Greek philosophy, but the concept is biblical in the sense that God imposed
order (Gen. 1: 2). Furthermore, there is no suggestion that the
origin of evil is matter but simply that God created 'all things
that they might have being' (1: 14). All creatures of the ani-
mal world, even the 'mere vermin' (verse 15), are God's. *thy
almighty hand*: *hand* means God, who is also called 'word'.
Both terms express God's power. In Isa. 48: 13 'hand' is
translated in the targum by 'word'. *almighty* is used here and
in 18: 15 in the phrase 'almighty Word'.

18–20. The real question is why God made use of 'mere

vermin' when he had so many fiercer animals as agents of divine vengeance. The answer is in the phrase *by measure and number and weight*. God is bound by the same principles he used in creating the world and so, as verse 16 tells us, 'the instruments of a man's sin are the instruments of his punishment'. The Egyptians are said to have worshipped 'mere vermin' and so that is their downfall. The phrases *single breath* and *breath of thy power* are synonyms for God.

21. The idea that God is omnipotent is the basis for what has just been said. Earlier it was argued that God was omniscient and omnipresent (cp. 1: 7).

22. *the whole world is like a grain...or a drop of dew*: the passage reflects the thought of Isa. 40: 12–21 where by a series of rhetorical questions the insignificance of man before the creator God is underlined. The simile is especially like that in the Septuagint of Isa. 40: 15 'no more than moisture on the scales'. Combining this with 'measure' and 'weight' in verse 20 the writer intended to stress the exceeding smallness of the world and the refined delicacy of God's equity.

23–5. *thou art merciful*: the omnipotent God is a source of mercy and forgiveness in order to effect repentance, rather than blind might. This same argument is put forward in 2 Pet. 3: 9 'It is not that the Lord is slow in fulfilling his promise...but that he is very patient...because it is not his will for any to be lost, but for all to come to repentance.' *all existing things are dear to thee* expresses the argument of 1: 14. Even in 12: 10–11 the wicked were given 'space for repentance' even though there was 'a curse on their race from the beginning'.

These two views of the nature of evil are found in the Old Testament. Hosea saw Israel as initially innocent but becoming spoiled in the wilderness. Ezekiel, on the other hand, saw Israel as the child of a mixed marriage. Probably 11: 24 is truer than 12: 10–11. Certainly the writer of Wisdom developed the argument that all things are dear to God because God's 'imperishable breath' (12: 1) is in them all. The writer used such vocabulary as God's *will, called into being* by God to buttress his argument. Since 'imperishable breath' is a synonym for God the writer had a Hebraic view of spirit as the creative power of God.

26. The phrase *lovest all that lives* is an example of the author's misuse of a Greek word. The Greek actually means 'loving one's own life too well', i.e. being a coward, which is hardly a description appropriate to God. The author meant that God is one who loves the living. ✻

GOD'S JUDGEMENT TEMPERED WITH MERCY

2 For this reason thou dost correct offenders little by little, admonishing them and reminding them of their sins, in order that they may leave their evil ways and put their
3 trust, O Lord, in thee. For example, the ancient inhabi-
4 tants of thy holy land were hateful to thee for their loath-
5 some practices, their sorcery and unholy rites, ruthless murders of children, cannibal feasts of human flesh and
6 blood; they were initiates of a secret ritual in which parents slaughtered their defenceless children. Therefore it was thy will to destroy them at the hand of our fore-
7 fathers, so that the land which is of all lands most precious in thine eyes could receive in God's children settlers worthy
8 of it. And yet thou didst spare their lives because even they were men, sending hornets as the advance-guard of thy
9 army to exterminate them gradually. It was well within thy power to let the godly overwhelm the godless in a pitched battle, or to wipe them out in an instant with
10 cruel beasts or by one stern word. But thou didst carry out their sentence gradually to give them space for repent-ance, knowing well enough that they came of evil stock,

their wickedness ingrained, and that their way of thinking would not change to the end of time, for there was 11 a curse on their race from the beginning.

Nor was it out of deference to anyone else that thou gavest them an amnesty for their misdeeds; for to thee no 12 one can say 'What hast thou done?' or dispute thy verdict. Who shall bring a charge against thee for destroying nations which were of thy own making? Who shall appear against thee in court to plead the cause of guilty men? For there is no other god but thee; all the world is 13 thy concern, and there is none to whom thou must prove the justice of thy sentence. There is no king or other ruler 14 who can outface thee on behalf of those whom thou hast punished. But thou art just and orderest all things justly, 15 counting it alien to thy power to condemn a man who ought not to be punished. For thy strength is the source of 16 justice, and it is because thou art master of all that thou sparest all. Thou showest thy strength when men doubt 17 the perfection of thy power; it is when they know it and yet are insolent that thou dost punish them. But thou, 18 with strength at thy command, judgest in mercy and rulest us in great forbearance; for the power is thine to use when thou wilt.

✴ 2. *For this reason*: God is merciful because his 'imperishable breath' is in all things and he is anxious for the wicked to repent. God's mercy stems from his creative power (11: 23 – 12: 1) and God's mercy and justice stem from his restraint in exercising his power (12: 15–17). Two cases are studied: as an example of God's power, the Canaanites (12: 3–14) and as an example of God's mercy and justice, the Israelites (12: 19–22).

Moderation towards the Canaanites: because God is merciful (11: 23) he corrects *offenders little by little*. God's concern is that none 'go astray' (6: 9) but when they fall, as Adam did, then God stands by man (10: 1). Such concern is because God 'takes no pleasure in the destruction of any living thing' (1: 13). The idea that the correction takes place *little by little* is a frequent theme here: 'gradually' (verses 8, 10), 'space for repentance' (verse 10), 'time and space to get free of their wickedness' (verse 20). The explanation for God's patience is found in Exod. 23: 29–30: 'I will not drive them out all in one year, or the land would become waste and the wild beasts too many for you.' Also the writer was demonstrating his universalism by stressing not only his interest in Israel but his concern for the Canaanite sinner.

3–6. *For example* (cp. 'By acts like these', 12: 19): the first case to be cited, *the ancient inhabitants of thy holy land*: the Canaanites. The phrase *holy land* is familiar to-day, from medieval times, but only twice in the Old Testament and never in the New. The Canaanites *were hateful to thee*. Although God hates nothing he has created (11: 24), he cannot tolerate either the sinner or the evil deed (cp. 14: 8–9). In Hos. 9: 15 we find the same idea – 'their wickedness was seen at Gilgal; there did I hate them'. Hateful to God then are their *loathsome practices*, which are subsequently delineated: (1) *sorcery* which, by means of the superstitious use of drugs, etc., worked magic (cp. Deut. 18: 10); (2) *unholy rites* such as forcing children to walk through fire to Molech (cp. Deut 12: 31 'they even burn their sons and their daughters'); (3) *ruthless murders of children* such as Jephthah's daughter (Judg. 11: 39) or Mesha's son (2 Kings 3: 27); (4) *cannibal feasts of human flesh and blood*: the author may be exaggerating since there is no biblical evidence; (5) *initiates of a secret ritual*: although the term 'initiates' may suggest a borrowing from Greek vocabulary, since the writer intended to associate the religious practice of the Canaanites with those more infamous rituals of the hellenistic mystery religions, the term is actually found elsewhere, in the Septuagint.

6. Because of the great wickedness of the Canaanites *it was thy will to destroy them at the hand of our forefathers*: that is, the Israelites who were led from Egypt. There are three biblical reasons why God willed the destruction of the Canaanites, and the writer added one of his own (verse 7). In the Old Testament God wanted the inhabitants of Canaan destroyed because he loved Israel, or because the wickedness of the Canaanites was so great, or because the Canaanites might have taught the Israelites abominable things. Here in addition, the writer developed the idea of colonization ('settlers', verse 7) which is suggested by 'bring you in to give you their land' (Deut. 4: 38). Because it is a new idea the writer drew on the language of classical Greek to describe the act. Then, because the same Greek words appeared in the Septuagint of Jer. 29: 1 to describe the exiles in Babylon who were to return to the promised land, the writer thought of the Israelites coming out of Egypt as colonists.

8. *thou didst spare their lives*: the author re-affirmed his basic thesis that man is created for life, not death (1: 14; 11: 23–4). God sent *hornets*, i.e. a destruction or peril to exterminate, gradually allowing time for repentance.

9. God has the power to destroy (but it is tempered with mercy) in *battle* (cp. Amalekites in Exod. 17 or Ai in Josh. 8); *with cruel beasts*; or *by one stern word* (18: 15 the 'almighty Word' is described as a 'relentless warrior'). The annihilation could happen *in an instant* in contrast to 'little by little' (12: 2).

10–11*a*. The fact that there was *a curse on their race from the beginning* is a further reason for God to show his patience. Canaan was cursed by Noah because Canaan had seen his father's nakedness. The writer was arguing historically here, basing his argument on the biblical belief (cp. Gen. 9: 24–7) that all the nations except the Jews were naturally evil.

Despite the fact that Augustine quoted this verse as proof of original sin there is no such theological connotation here. In 11: 23–5 the writer has already stated two possible explanations for the origin of evil. He still held to the thesis that God did not intend death, otherwise there would be no need for any *space for repentance.*

11–15. *Nor was it out of deference to anyone else that thou gavest them an amnesty for their misdeeds;...For there is no other god but thee;... There is no king...who can outface thee*: although God is not answerable to anyone, still he is just. In Gen. 18: 25 the question is asked, 'Shall not the judge of all the earth do what is just?'

16–17. Verse 16 introduces the reason for God's mercy and justice: his strength and sovereignty. *strength* and *power* (verse 17) are used in the opposite sense to that in 2: 11 where the wicked consider that righteousness gives way to power in an evil sense. Punishment comes to those who *know* God's power and *are insolent*. In Exod. 5: 2 Pharaoh asks: '"Who is the LORD?"...I care nothing for the LORD: and I tell you I will not let Israel go.' However, the argument in this section can equally well refer to everyman who knows and remains *insolent*.

18. Although God has *strength at* his *command*, he rules us *in great forbearance*. God is not indifferent but is guided by his love for his creatures. Ps. 78: 38–9 reflects the sense of this passage:

> Yet he wiped out their guilt...
> often he restrained his wrath
> and did not rouse his anger to its height.
> He remembered that they were only mortal men.

God has the power to use when he will as Ps. 115: 3 says: 'Our God is in high heaven; he does whatever pleases him.' *

MERCY AND JUDGEMENT

19 By acts like these thou didst teach thy people that the just man must also be kind-hearted, and thou hast filled thy sons with hope by the offer of repentance for their
20 sins. If thou didst use such care and such indulgence even

in punishing thy children's enemies, who deserved to die, granting them time and space to get free of their wickedness, with what discrimination thou didst pass judgement 21 on thy sons, to whose fathers thou hast given sworn covenants full of the promise of good!

So we are chastened by thee, but our enemies thou dost 22 scourge ten thousand times more, so that we may lay thy goodness to heart when we sit in judgement, and may hope for mercy when we ourselves are judged. This is why 23 the wicked who had lived their lives in heedless folly were tormented by thee with their own abominations. They 24 had strayed far down the paths of error, taking for gods the most contemptible and hideous creatures, deluded like thoughtless children. And so, as though they were 25 mere babes who have not learnt reason, thou didst visit on them a sentence that made them ridiculous; but those 26 who do not take warning from such derisive correction will experience the full weight of divine judgement. They 27 were indignant at their own sufferings, but finding themselves chastised through the very creatures they had taken to be gods, they recognized that the true God was he whom they had long ago refused to know. Thus the full rigour of condemnation descended on them.

✶ 19–27. In verses 19–21 God's mercy toward Israel is stressed. In verses 22–7 the inevitability of God's judgement is underlined.

19. *thou didst teach thy people*: Israel learns by acts like these that God's sovereign power is merciful and righteous and also that God prefers a man to repent rather than be punished. *kind-hearted*: i.e. a lover of man. This is an attribute which wisdom also possesses. The just man is to imitate wisdom and

possess the same quality. In this is one of the writer's truest anticipations of the New Testament: Matt. 5: 43 'Love your neighbour.'

20–1. A comparison in the rabbinic style, based on the literary convention of the comparison of the less and the more important: 'if such happens...how much more...': if God shows *such care and such indulgence* for the Canaanites then how much more for Israel, the chosen. *care* and *indulgence* are synonyms expressing God's infinite patience as expressed in *time and space to get free of their wickedness*, referring to the Canaanites. Such an idea is common in the Old Testament with reference to Israel. The new emphasis here is the extension of God's patience to pagan peoples. God then acts toward Israel with *discrimination*, i.e. carefulness. The *fathers* with whom *covenants* have been sworn are Abraham, Isaac, and Jacob.

22. *chastened...scourge*: these two terms stress the difference between the correction meted out to the righteous (cp. 3: 5; 6: 11 ('so you will learn'); 11: 9 ('discipline')) and to the ungodly (cp. 16: 16). As in Deut. 8: 5 'God was disciplining (chastening)' his people 'as a father disciplines his son'; although the two words appear in Prov. 3: 11–12 ('do not spurn the LORD's correction (chastening)...he punishes (scourges) a favourite son') the background of the argument is in Ps. 32: 10 ('Many are the torments of the ungodly; but unfailing love enfolds him who trusts in the LORD'). *ten thousand times more* stresses the quality of God's judgement on the enemy who experience his wrath and the 'full weight' and 'full rigour' of his judgement (verses 26–7).

23. The author alluded to the Egyptians and re-stated the principle expressed in 11: 16. *abominations* are idols (14: 11).

24. Because the Egyptians practised idolatry they must be punished. The argument here is leading to the long digression on idolatry in chs. 13–15; *contemptible and hideous creatures* (cp. 11: 15–16).

26. *warning from such derisive correction* means that as child's

play is to man's work so were the earlier chastisements to God's real judgements.

27. The argument of this verse is already found in 11: 13. *Thus the full rigour of condemnation descended on them*: even though the Egyptians finally acknowledged God they still refused to let Israel go, and so they experienced the *full rigour*, i.e. the death of the first-born and the drowning in the Red Sea. In 1 Thess. 2: 16 we find the same argument: 'All this time they have been making up the full measure of their guilt, and now retribution has overtaken them.' *they recognized that the true God was he whom they had long ago refused to know*: this provides the proper conclusion to ch. 12 and at the same time introduces chs. 13–15. For the author of Wisdom the refusal to acknowledge God brought suffering and death upon man. The thesis is fully delineated in the following section on idolatry. ✳

The evils of idolatry

FOOLS ARE THEY THAT PRACTISE NATURE WORSHIP

WHAT BORN FOOLS all men were who lived in **13** ignorance of God, who from the good things before their eyes could not learn to know him who really is, and failed to recognize the artificer though they observed his works! Fire, wind, swift air, the circle of the starry signs, 2 rushing water, or the great lights in heaven that rule the world – these they accounted gods. If it was through 3 delight in the beauty of these things that men supposed them gods, they ought to have understood how much better is the Lord and Master of it all; for it was by the prime author of all beauty that they were created. If it 4 was through astonishment at their power and influence,

men should have learnt from these how much more
5 powerful is he who made them. For the greatness and
beauty of created things give us a corresponding idea of
6 their Creator. Yet these men are not greatly to be blamed,
for when they go astray they may be seeking God and really
7 wishing to find him. Passing their lives among his works
and making a close study of them, they are persuaded by
8 appearances because what they see is so beautiful. Yet even
9 so they do not deserve to be excused, for with enough
understanding to speculate about the universe, why did
they not sooner discover the Lord and Master of it all?

✻ The thesis expressed in 12: 17, that the Egyptians, even
though they finally recognized the true God, must bear full
punishment for their deeds, is further developed in these
chapters by reference to nature worship and idolatry.

1. *Born fools...ignorance of God*: wisdom gives man knowledge of God (9: 13, 17). Since the whole book is about
acquiring wisdom the writer maintained that those who do not
are *fools* and 'degraded' (verse 10). The stress in this phrase is
on *fools* rather than *born* because the author believed that man
was made in the image of eternity (2: 23). Therefore, *born
fools* cannot mean original foolishness but rather a tendency
to waywardness developed by choice, as in Jer. 2: 5: 'What
fault did your forefathers find in me, that they wandered far
from me?' In contrast to those who get wisdom anyone who
cannot see God behind nature is a fool. He worships nature
and that kind of idolatry attaches to the worshipper, as
Jeremiah said, 'pursuing empty phantoms and themselves
becoming empty' (Jer. 2: 5). Man should have deduced God's
hand in *the good things before their eyes*. *good things*: creatures.
Ps. 19: 1 noted this fact:

> The heavens tell out the glory of God,
> the vault of heaven reveals his handiwork.

Here again, the writer combined the Greek view of observing a work, for instance nature, and enjoying the intrinsic value of the thing itself, with the Old Testament idea of actually seeing in creation the power and grandeur of God: 'how much better is the Lord and Master of it all' (verse 3). The writer was greatly indebted to Second Isaiah, who also found his people substituting the outward form for the inner truth about God. *him who really is* ('I AM; that is who I am' – Exod. 3: 14) is parallel to *the artificer*, which implies that God is the craftsman. Jesus made use of the same combination when he used such expressions as 'I am the good shepherd'.

2. The deification of the various natural elements was extensively practised in the hellenistic world. Philo wrote: 'Some have deified the four elements, earth, water, air, and fire and others the sun and moon and stars...and the Creator, Governor, and Director they have obscured behind their false ascriptions.'

3–5. If these men worshipped a thing because of its *beauty* or *power and influence* or *greatness*, in the sense of magnitude, how much more they should have worshipped him who created it all.

6–7. *these men*: idolaters. *not greatly to be blamed*: to worship something that God has made is not as reprehensible as the worship of something man-made. When one contemplates a beautiful sunset or an outstanding piece of art the viewer often forgets the primary cause of the thing contemplated. There is a danger of men overlooking the truth when *Passing their lives among his works*.

8–9. *Yet even so*: although being misled is easy nevertheless *why did they not sooner discover?* They had *enough understanding* to consider the world and its ways. It is therefore ironic that men should fail to draw the logical conclusion of a *Lord and Master*. The author again underlined the basic short-coming or limitation of man without wisdom. He was made for eternity, 'but'. In the New Testament, Acts 17: 27–31 utilizes the same idea of man overlooking God in considering his creation. However, Acts added a new dimension: 'but now he commands mankind, all men everywhere, to repent, because he has fixed the day on which he will have the world judged' (verses 30–1). ✲

THE MOST DEGRADED WORSHIP: IDOLS

10 The really degraded ones are those whose hopes are set on dead things, who give the name of gods to the work of human hands, to gold and silver fashioned by art into images of living creatures, or to a useless stone carved by
11 a craftsman long ago. Suppose some skilled woodworker fells with his saw a convenient tree and deftly strips off all the bark, then works it up elegantly into some vessel
12 suitable for everyday use; and the pieces left over from his
13 work he uses to cook his food, and eats his fill. But among the waste there is one useless piece, crooked and full of knots, and this he takes and carves to occupy his idle moments, and shapes it with leisurely skill into the image
14 of a human being; or else he gives it the form of some contemptible creature, painting it with vermilion and raddling its surface with red paint, so that every flaw in it
15 is painted over. Then he makes a suitable shrine for it and
16 fixes it on the wall, securing it with iron nails. It is he who has to take the precautions on its behalf to save it from falling, for he knows that it cannot fend for itself: it is
17 only an image, and needs help. Yet he prays to it about his possessions and his wife and children, and feels no
18 shame in addressing this lifeless object; for health he appeals to a thing that is feeble, for life he prays to a dead thing, for aid he implores something utterly incapable, for a prosperous journey something that has not even the use

of its legs; in matters of earnings and business and success   19
in handicraft he asks effectual help from a thing whose
hands are entirely ineffectual.

The man, again, who gets ready for a voyage, and plans **14**
to set his course through the wild waves, cries to a piece
of wood more fragile than the ship which carries him.
Desire for gain invented the ship, and the shipwright with   2
his wisdom built it;[a] but it is thy providence, O Father,   3
that is its pilot, for thou hast given it a pathway through
the sea and a safe course among the waves, showing that   4
thou canst save from every danger, so that even a man
without skill can put to sea. It is thy will that the things   5
made by thy wisdom should not lie idle; and therefore
men trust their lives even to the frailest spar, and passing
through the billows on a mere raft come safe to land.
Even in the beginning, when the proud race of giants was   6
being brought to an end, the hope of mankind escaped on
a raft and, piloted by thy hand, bequeathed to the world
a new breed of men. For a blessing is on the wooden   7
vessel through which right has prevailed; but the wooden   8
idol made by human hands is accursed, and so is its
maker – he because he made it, and the perishable thing
because it was called a god. Equally hateful to God are the   9
godless man and his ungodliness; the doer and the deed   10
shall both be punished.

And so retribution shall fall upon the idols of the heathen,   11
because though part of God's creation they have been
made into an abomination, to make men stumble and to
catch the feet of fools. The invention of idols is the root   12
of immorality; they are a contrivance which has blighted

[a] *Other witnesses read* and wisdom was the shipwright that built it.

13 human life. They did not exist from the beginning, nor
14 will they be with us for ever; superstition brought them
into the world, and for good reason a short sharp end is in
store for them.

✶ The author's position in condemning idolatry is found
both in Jewish and Greek writings. The whole section is un-
original, borrowing heavily from the Old Testament for both
imagery and vocabulary. Such series of antitheses as are set
up here were common in Greek rhetorical writing but also
found in the Old Testament.

10–14. *The really degraded* are those who rely on impotent
idols. Isa. 44: 9–20 contains a description of idol-making and
presumably was the author's immediate source; *the work of
human hands*: idols. There is much irony in these verses, as
there is in Isa. 44: 9ff. A *skilled* worker made an ineffective
idol in his leisure time from the *waste* of a *useless piece*, *crooked
and full of knots*. The result is an idol either of a human model
or some contemptible creature.

15–16. The irony continues to underline this idol's inability to do what its creator wants: he fixed it firmly to the
wall *to save it from falling*.

17–19. Although he prayed to it for help, it was the one
who needed to be helped. The suggestion of an ineffective
idol draws heavily on Ps. 115. Such phrases as *lifeless object,
a dead thing, has not even the use of its legs, entirely ineffectual*,
underline the writer's point and heighten the irony.

14: 1–11. In the following section idolaters are further
condemned.

1–2. *a piece of wood more fragile than the ship*: three contrasts
emphasize how much better the ship is than the idol that man
values: (1) the wood for the idol was less strong than that for
the ship, (2) the ship was built with human wisdom while the
idol was made in the craftsman's leisure time (cp. 13: 11, 13),
(3) man built the ship but God's providence guided it.

3–5. Even though the best of human wisdom has built the ship it is God's providence which was *its pilot*. The Greek word for *providence* appears here and in 17: 2 for the first time in the Greek Bible. The term is borrowed from Greek literary and philosophical writings but the idea belongs to the Old Testament as expressed in Ps. 145: 9 'The LORD is good to all men, and his tender care rests upon all his creatures.' *providence* for the writer was the logical extension of his theological position that God 'created all things that they might have being' (1: 13). The idea is of *providence* as a dynamic force for it is the *pilot*. *a pathway through the sea* and *a safe course among the waves* demonstrate Hebraic poetic form and also reflect the literary influence of Ps. 77: 19–20 and Isa. 43: 16 and the thought itself concerns the safe conduct through the Red Sea, an idea further developed in verse 4.

In the phrase *the things made by thy wisdom should not lie idle* the stress is on *things made* and *idle*, suggesting that wisdom should produce results for man's benefit. The *frailest spar* and *mere raft* suggest the contrast between what man can build and the mighty sea.

6–7. Although unnamed, *the hope of mankind* is Noah and his family who sailed a *raft*, the term in Greek for any vessel which was not sound or built to a shipwright's specifications. The result of Noah's ark being *piloted* by God (*thy hand*) was a new breed of men (Gen. 9: 1 'Be fruitful...fill the earth'). Philo described the event in these words: 'Noah, counted worthy to be the beginning of a new generation.'

a blessing is on the wooden vessel: although some of the Church Fathers applied the phrase to the wood of the Cross it only refers to Noah's ark. *right has prevailed*: the same Greek word as 'justice' (1: 1). Noah is called 'preacher of righteousness' in 2 Pet. 2: 5. This verse ends the ship metaphor.

8–10. The link between what precedes and follows is *wooden*. The writer continued the comparison by contrasting 'blessing' (verse 7) and *accursed*. It is true that a ship is also made with hands but the writer was emphasizing the fact that the Greek word (*made by human hands*) has become a technical term for idol.

The argument proceeds that *the doer and the deed* are one and the same. This thought is found in Jer. 2: 5, which says that the corruptness of the object is extended to the person who worships it. There is no way in semitic or Old Testament thought to separate the doer from his deed. Therefore if an idol is accursed so is its maker. In contrast to this total condemnation we note that God loves his creatures and wishes only life for them (11: 24–5).

11–14. *And so* introduces the conclusion to the discussion so far. *retribution* conveys a Hebrew idea which in this case means punishment (in 3: 13, 'at the great assize of souls...find a fruitfulness of her own', it meant 'blessing'). The reasons why punishment is inevitable are serious: (1) part of God's creation has been made an *abomination*, an idol; (2) idols *make men stumble*: they are a trap or snare; (3) they are *the root of immorality*: spiritual levity which led a man to abandon God for idols; (4) they are *a contrivance which has blighted human life*: they cause moral corruption.

In addition to these serious reasons for rejecting idols there is the basic fact that *They did not exist from the beginning*. They are transient, while God is from the beginning and exists forever. Isa. 2: 17–18 reads 'and the Lord alone shall be exalted on that day, while the idols shall pass away utterly'. ✻

THE ORIGIN OF IDOLATRY

15 Some father, overwhelmed with untimely grief for the child suddenly taken from him, made an image of the child and honoured thenceforth as a god what was once a dead human being, handing on to his household the
16 observance of rites and ceremonies. Then this impious custom, established by the passage of time, was observed as a law. Or again graven images came to be worshipped

at the command of despotic princes. When men could 17
not do honour to such a prince before his face because he
lived far away, they made a likeness of that distant face,
and produced a visible image of the king they sought to
honour, eager to pay court to the absent prince as though
he were present. Then the cult grows in fervour as those 18
to whom the king is unknown are spurred on by ambi-
tious craftsmen. In his desire, it may be, to please the 19
monarch, a craftsman skilfully distorts the likeness into
an ideal form, and the common people, beguiled by the 20
beauty of the workmanship, take for an object of worship
him whom lately they honoured as a man. So this becomes 21
a trap for living men: enslaved by mischance or mis-
government, men confer on stocks and stones the name
that none may share.

Then, not content with gross error in their knowledge 22
of God, men live in the constant warfare of ignorance and
call this monstrous evil peace. They perform ritual mur- 23
ders of children and secret ceremonies and the frenzied
orgies of unnatural cults; the purity of life and marriage 24
is abandoned; and a man treacherously murders his
neighbour or corrupts his wife and breaks his heart. All is 25
in chaos – bloody murder, theft and fraud, corruption,
treachery, riot, perjury, honest men driven to distraction; 26
ingratitude, moral corruption, sexual perversion, break-
down of marriage, adultery, debauchery. For the wor- 27
ship of idols, whose names it is wrong even to mention,
is the beginning, cause, and end of every evil. Men either 28
indulge themselves to the point of madness, or produce
inspired utterance which is all lies, or live dishonest lives,
or break their oath without scruple. They perjure them- 29

selves and expect no harm because the idols they trust in
30 are lifeless. On two counts judgement will overtake them:
because in their devotion to idols they have thought
wrongly about God, and because, in their contempt for
31 religion, they have deliberately perjured themselves. It is
not any power in what they swear by, but the nemesis of
sin, that always pursues the transgression of the wicked.

✳ The idolatrous aberration manifests itself in three ways. The
first two ways circulated widely in the hellenistic world. The
third was added by the writer himself.

15–16 a. (1) The first cause is the father's affection for a de-
ceased son.

15. *the observance of rites and ceremonies* suggest that we are
concerned with more than the private worship of a dead child.
Possibly the author was thinking of the cult developed in
honour of famous men. The vocabulary, borrowed from the
mystery cults, is that used in honouring a new god.

16. *this impious custom...observed as a law* refers to the
practice of child veneration which in the first place was personal and private but soon was enforced by a ruler on his
subjects (*at the command of despotic princes*).

17–18. (2) The second idolatrous way is that of honouring
a ruler by erecting a statue *to the absent prince as though he were
present*. This was a very common practice in the hellenistic
world.

19–20. (3) The writer's own third idolatrous way which
proceeds naturally from the first two: the craftsman, wishing
to please his ruler, skilfully shaped *the likeness* into a most
beautiful *form*. The Greek idea of worshipping beauty for its
own intrinsic worth was rejected in the Old Testament because the making of a carved image was specifically prohibited
(Exod. 20: 4). The writer scorned the whole practice of idolatry which led man to worship *an object* rather than the truth
the object was made to represent.

21. *So this becomes a trap*: *this* refers to child-worship and ruler-worship. These practices were a *trap for living men*. *the name that none may share* is God's name, as Isa. 42: 8 says: 'I am the LORD; the LORD is my name; I will not give my glory to another god, nor my praise to any idol.'

22-6. The consequences of idolatry (verses 22-31) result from the fact that, true to human nature, men were *not content* to be ignorant of God. They dared to call the idol (*this monstrous evil*) peace. In Jer. 6: 14 the people call, 'All is well', in ignorance of the true facts. Verses 23-6 record a long list of immoralities such as are found in Hos. 4: 2. The *ritual murders of children* refers to Molech worship (cp. 12: 5); *frenzied orgies*: Bacchanalian celebrations of the mystery cults. The writer also listed the decline of respect for the individual (*murder, perjury*, etc.) and the rejection of the sanctity of marriage (*adultery, sexual perversion*, etc.).

27-9. *For* introduces the reasons why idolatry is wrong: it is (1) *the beginning, cause, and end of every evil*; (2) *Men either indulge themselves to the point of madness* ('frenzied orgies'); or, (3) *produce inspired utterance which is all lies* ('perjury'); (4) men *live dishonest lives*; (5) they *break their oath*: the Jews considered that an oath made to an idol was not binding. We can find all these results of idolatry also described in Jer. 5.

30-1. These verses restate the basic premise: *because...they have thought wrongly about God, and because...they have deliberately perjured themselves, judgement* is inevitable and the punishment fits the crime (cp. 11: 16). ✳

ISRAEL IS NOT IDOLATROUS

But thou, our God, art kind and true and patient, **15** a merciful ruler of all that is. For even if we sin, we are 2 thine; we acknowledge thy power. But we will not sin, because we know that we are accounted thine. To know 3 thee is the whole of righteousness, and to acknowledge

4 thy power is the root of immortality. We have not been
led astray by the perverted inventions of human skill or
the barren labour of painters, by some gaudy painted shape,
5 the sight of which arouses in fools a passionate desire for a
6 mere image without life or breath. They are in love with
evil and deserve to trust in nothing better, those who do
these evil things or hanker after them or worship them.

✿ 1. *But thou* contrasts the living God with the lifeless idol in
the phrase 'any power in what they swear by' (14: 31). God's
nature is *kind* as in Exod. 34: 6 'a god compassionate and
gracious, long-suffering, ever constant and true'; *true* in the
biblical sense of constant, immutable to decisions, and *patient*.

2–3. These verses should be read together in order to
appreciate the inverted arrangement of the thoughts as sometimes occurs in Hebrew poetry: *For even if we sin...we acknowledge thy power/and to acknowledge thy power is...immortality*
and *But we will not sin, because...accounted thine/ To know thee is
the whole of righteousness.* Otherwise, from verse 2 alone we
might conclude that the wicked are to be punished and God's
people protected no matter what they would do. Instead the
writer continued his thought on the power and mercy of God
in contrast to the idols. *even if we sin* God's mercy will remain
because *we acknowledge* his *power.* And, to *acknowledge thy power*
is the *root of immortality.* However, *we will not sin* because we
know we are God's and *to know* God *is the whole of righteousness.*

The thought for the argument in these verses is found in such
Old Testament passages as Jer. 9: 23–4:

> Let not the wise man boast of his wisdom
>   nor the valiant of his valour;
> let not the rich man boast of his riches;
>   but if any man would boast, let him boast of this,
>   that he understands and knows me.
> For I am the LORD, I show unfailing love.

4–5. The phrase *We have not been led astray* by the idols shows the concern uppermost in the writer's mind because of the times in which the Jews lived, in exile from Palestine. He suggested that since the exile in Babylon the Jews have been monotheists. Such Greek practice as worshipping a *gaudy painted shape* (cp. 13: 14) has not tempted the faithful Jew. The writer also emphasized the contrast between the idol as *a mere image without life or breath* with God 'who really is' (13: 1) and whose 'imperishable breath' is in all (12: 1).

6. A conclusion to 15: 1–5, and an introduction to the discussion of the folly of idol-makers, revealing how much they desire to make their images, how they *hanker after them*, and *worship them*. In these words we find a summary of the results of idolatry.   ✳

THE FOLLY OF IDOL-MAKERS AND OF THE EGYPTIANS

For a potter kneading his clay laboriously moulds every 7 vessel for our use, but out of the self-same clay he fashions without distinction the pots that are to serve for honourable uses and the opposite; and what the purpose of each one is to be, the moulder of the clay decides. And then 8 with ill-directed toil he makes a false god out of the same clay, this man who not long before was himself fashioned out of earth and soon returns to the place whence he was taken, when the living soul that was lent to him must be repaid. His concern is not that he must one day fall sick 9 or that his span of life is short; but he must vie with goldsmiths and silversmiths and copy the bronze-workers, and he thinks it does him credit to make counterfeits. His 10 heart is ashes, his hope worth less than common earth, and his life cheaper than his own clay, because he did not 11 recognize by whom he himself was moulded, or who it was that inspired him with an active soul and breathed

12 into him the breath of life. No, he reckons our life a game, and our existence a market where money can be made; 'one must get a living', he says, 'by fair means or foul'.

13 But this man knows better than anyone that he is doing wrong, this maker of fragile pots and idols from the same earthy stuff.

14 The greatest fools of all, and worse than infantile, were

15 the enemies and oppressors of thy people, for they supposed all their heathen idols to be gods, although they have eyes that cannot see, nostrils that cannot draw breath, ears that cannot hear, fingers that cannot feel, and

16 feet that are useless for walking. It was a man who made them; one who draws borrowed breath gave them their shape. But no human being has the power to shape a god

17 like himself: he is only mortal, but what he makes with his impious hands is dead; and so he is better than the objects of his worship, for he is at least alive – they never can be.

18 Moreover, these men worship animals, the most revolting animals. Compared with the rest of the brute

19 creation, their divinities are the least intelligent. Even as animals they have no beauty to make them desirable; when God approved and blessed his work, they were left out.

* The writer who had condemned the idol now turns his words on the idol-maker. While in 13: 11ff. there was a description of the making of a wooden idol, here it is the potter's activities which are discussed. The depth of the writer's contempt for the potter's work is threefold:

7–8. (1) The potter shapes out of the *self-same clay* pots for sacred (*honourable*) and profane (*opposite*) uses *And then...* *makes a false god out of the same clay* with *ill-directed toil*. All these terms are used contemptuously. For instance, *ill-directed toil* can be understood when related to *laboriously* and 'perverted inventions of human skill' (verse 4). The whole effort is misguided and evil. The author passed judgement when he wrote (verse 16) 'no human being has the power to shape a god like himself'. Furthermore, the *self-same clay* is used for pots and gods just as the wood-worker made his god out of discarded pieces of wood.

(2) The writer was contemptuous of the potter because he put himself on a par with God, who shaped man from clay (Gen. 2: 7). Isa. 45: 9 asks the same question:

> Will the pot contend with the potter,
> or the earthenware with the hand that shapes it?

The irony of the imperfection of the potter's god is heightened by the fact that *the living soul that was lent to him* (the potter) *must be repaid*. 'active soul' and 'breath of life' (verse 11) are synonyms for the divine loan as expressed in 8: 19. The thought is purely Old Testament.

9–12. (3) The writer condemned the potter for ignoring his end (*he must one day fall sick*) and judgement (*his span of life is short*) and expending his energy in the manufacture of counterfeit gods for profit. The potter's *life* is *cheaper than his own clay* because he failed to equate his own frail nature with the fragile material with which he was working. Furthermore, *His heart is ashes* as the Septuagint of Isa. 44: 20 says. The idea that *life* was *a game*, and the emphasis on profit, were current concepts in the writer's day. As we can see these arguments run counter to the Hebraic concept of man and so are rejected by the writer.

14. The author of Wisdom concluded his discourse on idolatry (12: 27ff.) by singling out the Egyptians (*the enemies and oppressors of thy people*). He did not name them, possibly

because he was living among them. Everyone knows they 'worship animals' (verse 18) which is the lowest form of idolatry (*worse than infantile*), and 'most revolting' (verse 18). The *oppressors of thy people* were the pharaoh of Egypt at the time of the exodus and now probably also the contemporary rulers, who have been variously identified. If positive identification were possible then we could date this book precisely. However, for the writer's purpose specific identification was not essential.

15. This verse discusses again (cp. 13: 16–19) the idea of an impotent idol.

16–17. Underlines again (cp. verse 9) that mortal man (7: 1; 9: 14 'feeble') can only create a dead thing (13: 10, 18; 15: 5). However, man is *better* than the idol he made because *he is at least alive*.

18–19. Suggests the animals themselves are both *revolting* (11: 15) and *the least intelligent*. Finally, in God's approving of his creation, *they were left out*. This is not strictly true since only the serpent was so condemned (Gen. 3: 14–15) and, not even it, before the Fall. ✳

The pattern of divine justice

✳ Divine justice with regard to Egypt and Israel is resumed in a further five 'contrasts', drawn from the period of the wanderings in the wilderness, which complete the study begun at 11: 5–14: (1) 16: 1–14, animals; (2) 16: 15–29, the elements; (3) 17: 1 – 18: 4, darkness; (4) 18: 5–25, death; and (5) 19: 1–21, the Red Sea. The same thesis of 'measure for measure' (11: 5, 16) is used in these sections, as well as the idea that even Israel must be punished, but in mercy (11: 9). In the following verses we shall note a number of instances where the writer revised the biblical text to suit his purpose. ✳

THE SECOND 'CONTRAST' BETWEEN EGYPT AND ISRAEL: ANIMALS

AND SO THE OPPRESSORS were fittingly chastised by **16** creatures like these: they were tormented by swarms of vermin. But while they were punished, thou didst make 2 provision for thy people, sending quails for them to eat, an unwonted food to satisfy their hunger; for thy purpose 3 was that whereas those others, hungry as they were, should turn in loathing even from necessary food because the creatures sent upon them were so disgusting, thy people after a short spell of scarcity should enjoy unwonted delicacies. It was right that the scarcity falling on 4 the oppressors should be inexorable, and that thy people should learn by brief experience how their enemies were tormented. Even when fierce and furious snakes attacked 5 thy people and the bites of writhing serpents were spreading death, thy anger did not continue to the bitter end; their short trouble was sent them as a lesson, and they 6 were given a symbol[a] of salvation to remind them of the requirements of thy law. For any man who turned to- 7 wards it was saved, not by the thing he looked upon but by thee, the saviour of all. In this way thou didst convince 8 our enemies that thou art the deliverer from every evil. Those other men died from the bite of locusts and flies, 9 and no remedy was found to save their lives, because it was fitting for them to be chastised by such creatures. But 10 thy sons did not succumb to the fangs of snakes, however venomous, because thy mercy came to their aid and healed them. It was to remind them of thy utterances that 11

[a] Or pledge.

they were bitten and quickly recovered; it was for fear
they might fall into deep forgetfulness and become un-
12 responsive to thy kindness. For it was neither herb nor
poultice that cured them, but thy all-healing word,
13 O Lord. Thou hast the power of life and death, thou
bringest a man down to the gates of death and up again.
14 Man in his wickedness may kill, but he cannot bring back
the breath of life that has gone forth nor release a soul that
death has arrested.

✵ 1. *swarms of vermin*: as in 11: 15, where this subject had
already been introduced, the author suggested that these were
the 'revolting animals' which Egypt worshipped (15: 18).
And so, in accordance with 11: 16, the Egyptians were punished by the very things through which they had sinned. In
contrast, according to 11: 5, these became a blessing for Israel:
namely, quails and serpents.

The author of Wisdom was taking liberties with the Old
Testament in order to underline his thesis. There is no Old
Testament evidence that the Egyptians worshipped frogs, lice,
flies or locusts. At the same time there is no biblical proof that
quails and serpents harmed only Egypt and benefited only
Israel. In actual fact, the plagues of vermin (Exod. 8: 7–28;
10: 4–19) did not destroy the Egyptians but only made life
miserable. Only in Ps. 78: 42–53 and 105: 26–42 is there expressed the idea that these minor plagues destroyed the
Egyptians.

The 'contrast' is heightened by the use of the vocabulary
designating Egypt – *oppressors*, 'those others' (verse 3), 'Those
other men' (verse 9) – and Israel – 'thy people' (verse 2),
'thy sons' (verse 10). Clearly the writer was on Israel's side.

2. *sending quails for them to eat, an unwonted food*: contrary to
Exod. 16: 8 'the LORD, in answer to your complaints, gives
you flesh to eat', this book ignores both the murmurings of

the people (Exod. 16: 2–8) and God's anger (Num. 11: 33–4; cp. Ps. 78: 30–1 'Yet they did not abandon their complaints even while the food was in their mouths. Then the anger of God blazed up against them').

3–4. *the creatures sent upon them were so disgusting*: the Egyptians, although starving, could not eat vermin such as frogs sent in plagues. By contrast, the Israelites, *after a short spell of scarcity*, enjoyed *unwonted delicacies*. During the *spell of scarcity*, according to verse 4, the Israelites suffered minor discomfort from hunger, not as punishment, but to help them understand how much greater was the suffering of the Egyptians. This is the rabbinic argument of 'how much the more'. The verb *were tormented* in the Greek conveys the idea that the Egyptians and the Israelites suffered concurrently. How the Egyptians were tormented is spelled out in verses 8–9. The Israelites enjoyed *unwonted delicacies*. The author failed to mention Israel's gluttony (Num. 11: 32–3: 'busy gathering quails all that day, all night, and all next day...ten homers').

Verses 5–11 deal with snakes in the wilderness. Num. 21: 6–9 is the biblical source for this section which the writer has revised to suit his own purpose.

5. *fierce and furious snakes* are 'poisonous' in Num. 21: 6. (The writer was also using the vocabulary of Isa. 27: 1 for *writhing serpents*.) Nevertheless, God's *anger did not continue to the bitter end* because his 'mercy came to their aid and healed them' (verse 10) in contrast to the ungodly who 'were pursued by pitiless anger to the bitter end' (19: 1).

6. *a symbol of salvation* refers to the 'bronze serpent' which Moses made (Num. 21: 9). Contrary to the biblical version, it had no intrinsic value in itself because God was 'the saviour of all' (verse 7). Some of the targums to Num. 21: 6 note that when gazing on the bronze serpent 'if the sufferer's heart was intent upon the name of the word of the Lord he lived' (cp. John 3: 14 'This Son of Man must be lifted up...so that everyone who has faith in him may in him possess eternal life'). *to remind them of the requirements of thy law*: the serpent as

a symbol of salvation was to remind Israel lest 'they might fall into deep forgetfulness and become unresponsive to thy kindness' (verse 11). It also proved to Egypt that God was 'the deliverer from every evil' (verse 8) and was punishing her justly (verse 9).

9–10. The study in 'contrasts' continues. The Egyptians are killed by animals that are not normally known to kill while the Israelites survive the bite of the serpent, usually considered fatal.

12. Continues the argument that any Israelite stung by the serpent was cured by *neither herb nor poultice* but by God's *word*, i.e. the all-powerful divine will. Here, as we have noted before, Hebraic thought does not distinguish between thought (word) and deed (action). Isa. 55: 10–11 expresses it well:

> and as the rain and the snow...
> ...do not return until they have watered the earth,
>   making it blossom and bear fruit,
> and give seed...
> so shall the word which comes from my mouth prevail;
>   it shall not return to me fruitless
> without accomplishing my purpose.

As far as the power of God's *word* is concerned, the fullest statement is to be found in 18: 15.

13–14. Further 'contrast' is expressed in God's ability to take and restore life, whereas man can only kill. The phrases *power of life and death* and *bringest a man down to the gates of death and up again* are synonyms. There is no suggestion of a resurrection in our sense, but only in Old Testament terms. The statement here sharpens and emphasizes the power of God over human destiny. The idea of restoring life may well be the same as that illustrated in the story of Elijah's restoration of life to the son of the widow of Zarephath (1 Kings 17: 17–23). ✳

THE THIRD 'CONTRAST' BETWEEN EGYPT AND ISRAEL: THE ELEMENTS

But from thy hand there is no escape; for godless men 15, 16
who refused to acknowledge thee were scourged by thy
mighty arm, pursued by extraordinary storms of rain and
hail in relentless torrents, and utterly destroyed by fire.
Strangest of all, in water, that quenches everything, the 17
fire burned more fiercely; creation itself fights to defend
the godly. At one time the flame was moderated, so that 18
it should not burn up the living creatures inflicted on the
godless, who were to learn from this that it was by God's
justice that they were pursued; at another time it blazed 19
even under water with more than the natural power of
fire, to destroy the produce of a sinful land. By contrast, 20
thy own people were given angels' food, and thou didst
send them from heaven, without labour of their own,
bread ready to eat, rich in delight of every kind and suited
to every taste. The sustenance thou didst supply showed 21
thy sweetness towards thy children, and the bread, serving
the desire of each man who ate it, was changed into what
he wished. Its snow and ice resisted fire and did not melt, 22
to teach them that whereas their enemies' crops had been
destroyed by fire that blazed in the hail and flashed
through the teeming rain, that same fire had now for- 23
gotten its own power, in order that the godly might be fed.

For creation, serving thee its maker, exerts its power 24
to punish the godless and relaxes into benevolence towards
those who trust in thee. And so it was at that time too: it 25
adapted itself endlessly in the service of thy universal
bounty, according to the desire of thy suppliants. So thy 26

sons, O Lord, whom thou hast chosen, were to learn that
it is not the growing of crops by which mankind is
nourished, but it is thy word that sustains those who trust
27 in thee. That substance, which fire did not destroy, simply
28 melted away when warmed by the sun's first rays, to teach
us that we must rise before the sun to give thee thanks and
29 pray to thee as daylight dawns. The hope of an ungrateful
man will melt like the hoar-frost of winter, and drain
away like water that runs to waste.

✳ 15–17. *no escape* from God; *thy hand, thy mighty arm* indicate
God's power; *scourged*: cp. 12: 22; *godless men who refused to
acknowledge thee*: cp. 12: 27; *extraordinary storms*: Exod. 9: 22ff.
speaks of the plague of hail. *water* and *fire* seem to unite to
punish the Egyptians. *creation*: nature (cp. 5: 17, 20; 16: 24;
19: 6).

18–19. Such phrases as *At one time, at another time*, 'By contrast' convey the dramatic sense of Egypt *versus* Israel. Also
the words *moderated* and *blazed*, which describe the flames,
emphasize the idea of destruction and beneficence, qualities
belonging to the nature of fire. In this section the writer
employed rhetorical exaggeration to make God's dealings
with the Egyptians appear more terrible.

20–3. The food for Israel is manna. The argument does not
follow the biblical record. The point the author was seeking to
underline was the 'contrast' between the destruction of 'the
produce of a sinful land' (verse 19) and the blessing obtained
by the 'angels' food' – most excellent food because food fit for
angels. The phrase refers to the manna in Exod. 16 and
Num. 11: 7–9. The targums to Numbers write 'the sons of
men ate bread that came down from the dwellings of the
angels'. This food is *bread ready to eat, bread serving the
desire of each man who ate it, snow and ice*, and 'universal
bounty' (verse 25).

20. *thou didst send* refers to Exod. 16: 4 where God rained down 'bread from heaven'. *without labour of their own*: that is, 'he gave them bread from heaven in plenty' (Ps. 105: 40). Another example of the way the writer coloured the exodus experience for his purpose is found in the phrase *suited to every taste* which is a fact contrary to that expressed in Num. 11: 6 and 21: 5 where it is recorded that they hated the manna.

21. *The sustenance* conveys the idea both of the manna being a revelation of God's mercy and of its fulfilling the people's needs.

22. The description of the manna as *snow and ice* (cp. 19: 21 'like ice'; and the Septuagint of Num. 11: 7 'the appearance of ice'; and Exod. 16: 14 'fine as hoar-frost') may also be dependent on Ps. 148: 8 'fire and hail, snow and ice'. In any case, the important point is the 'contrast' between the fire destroying the crops of Egypt and having no effect on the manna for the Israelites. In Exod. 16: 21 the sun melted the manna. For the idiom *fire that blazed in the hail* the writer was dependent on the Septuagint of Exod. 9: 24.

24–9. *exerts its power to punish the godless and relaxes into benevolence* enunciates again the general principle; the same element can punish and protect. *creation* means nature but especially fire. *exerts...relaxes* are terms used to describe the strings of a musical instrument (cp. 19: 18). In verse 25 nature is in *the service of* God's *universal bounty* (Ps. 104: 27 'All of them look expectantly to thee to give them their food at the proper time').

26. *thy sons, O Lord, whom thou hast chosen* is an idea common in the Old Testament. *it is not the growing of crops by which mankind is nourished, but it is thy word*: with the words *not... but*, possible both in Greek and in Hebrew, the writer sought to heighten the 'contrast' between the efforts of man and God's gift and thus to emphasize the power of God to sustain *those who trust in* him (cp. 16: 7, 12). In this instance it is the manna which is called *thy word*, which God sent down to his people. Here as in 16: 12 *thy word* is an expression of the all-

powerful divine will. In Matt. 4: 4 Jesus quoted the Old Testament to answer the devil: 'Man cannot live on bread alone; he lives on every word that God utters.' A similar view is expressed in Amos 8: 11: 'The time is coming...when I will send famine on the land, not hunger for bread...but for hearing the word of the LORD.'

27–8. Contrary to the suggestion in verse 23 that the manna was impervious to fire, here the writer reverted to the biblical text to indicate the time when man must pray to God. This is one of the most beautiful thoughts of the whole book. The thought of seeking God early in prayer is also biblical.

29. *The hope of an ungrateful man* melts and drains away. *ungrateful* is contrasted with 'give thee thanks' in verse 28. In Ps. 58: 6–7 is found the prayer

> Break, O LORD, the jaws of the unbelievers.
> May they melt, may they vanish like water. ✳

THE FOURTH 'CONTRAST' BETWEEN EGYPT AND ISRAEL: DARKNESS

17 Great are thy judgements and hard to expound; and
2 thus it was that uninstructed souls went astray. Thus heathen men imagined that they could lord it over thy holy people; but, prisoners of darkness and captives of unending night, they lay each immured under his own
3 roof, fugitives from eternal providence. Thinking that their secret sins might escape detection beneath a dark pall of oblivion, they lay in disorder, dreadfully afraid, terri-
4 fied by apparitions. For the dark corner that held them offered no refuge from fear, but loud unnerving noises roared around them, and phantoms with downcast un-
5 smiling faces passed before their eyes. No fire, however great, had force enough to give them light, nor had the

brilliant flaming stars strength to illuminate that hideous
darkness. There shone upon them only a blaze, of no 6
man's making, that terrified them, and in their panic they
thought the real world even worse than that imaginary
sight. The tricks of the sorcerers' art failed, and all their 7
boasted wisdom was exposed and put to shame; for the 8
very men who profess to drive away fear and trouble from
sick souls were themselves sick with dread that made them
ridiculous. Even if nothing frightful was there to terrify 9
them, yet having once been scared by the advancing
vermin and the hissing serpents, they collapsed in terror, 10
refusing even to look upon the air from which there can
be no escape.[a] For wickedness proves a cowardly thing 11
when condemned by an inner witness, and in the grip of
conscience gives way to forebodings of disaster. Fear is 12
nothing but an abandonment of the aid that comes from
reason; and hope, defeated by this inward weakness, 13
capitulates before ignorance of the cause by which the
torment comes.

So all that night, which really had no power against 14
them because it came upon them from the powerless
depths of hell, they slept the same haunted sleep, now 15
harried by portentous spectres, now paralysed by the
treachery of their own souls; sudden and unforeseen, fear
came upon them. Thus a man would fall down where he 16
stood and be held in durance, locked in a prison that had
no bars. Farmer or shepherd or labourer toiling in the 17
wilds, he was caught, and awaited the inescapable doom;
the same chain of darkness bound all alike. The whispering 18
breeze, the sweet melody of birds in spreading branches,

[a] *Or* there is no need to escape.

19 the steady beat of water that rushes by, the headlong crash of rocks falling, the racing of creatures as they bound along unseen, the roar of fierce wild beasts, or echo reverberating from hollows in the hills – all these sounds 20 paralysed them with fear. The whole world was bathed in the bright light of day, and went about its tasks un- 21 hindered; those men alone were overspread with heavy night, fit image of the darkness that awaited them; and heavier than the darkness was the burden each was to himself.

18   But for thy holy ones there shone a great light. And so their enemies, hearing their voices but not seeing them, counted them happy because they had not suffered like 2 themselves, gave thanks for their forbearance under provocation, and begged as a favour that they should part 3 company. Accordingly, thy gift was a pillar of fire to be the guide of their uncharted journey, a sun that would not 4 scorch them on their glorious expedition. Their enemies did indeed deserve to lose the light of day and be kept prisoners in darkness, for they had kept in durance thy sons, through whom the imperishable light of the law was to be given to the world.

✳ The writer based this fourth 'contrast', dealing with darkness, on the ninth plague (Exod. 10: 21–8). In ch. 17 and 18: 1–4 he considered the biblical statement that the plague was darkness to the Egyptians but light to the Israelites (Exod. 10: 23–4). The style of this fourth 'contrast' is different from the others in that the parallelism, familiar in Hebrew poetry and in most of the other sections of this book, is missing. Instead, the author drew on a highly developed Greek literary genre used to describe a descent into Hades. In this instance this sophisticated literary form is put at the service of Jewish eschatology. Greek moralists and jurists developed such a format for their discussions on the extent to which terror paralysed the guilty. It is this psychological analysis of fear (17: 11–13) which the writer developed in his exegesis of Exod. 10: 23–4.

The writer has allowed his imagination full rein in this 'contrast'. The biblical context remains but to it is added much more speculative and imaginative detail than in other sections of the book. ✻

PARALYSING FEAR

✻ 1–2. *Great are thy judgements*: a general statement related to the theme of ch. 16 'But from thy hand there is no escape' (16: 15). *judgements* are principles of justice, and they are *hard to expound*. The word is found nowhere else in the Septuagint but the thought is that of Ps. 92: 5–6:

> How great are thy deeds, O LORD!
> How fathomless thy thoughts!
> He who does not know this is a brute.

uninstructed souls: the Egyptians, who are called *heathen men, prisoners of darkness, captives of unending night*, and *fugitives from eternal providence*. With *prisoners of darkness* begins the interpretation of the concept of darkness as expressed in phrases in Exod. 10: 21–3: 'darkness that can be felt'; 'pitch dark'; 'Men could not see one another'; 'for three days no one stirred from where he was'. In verse 17 the writer called it 'the same chain of darkness'. In the following verses (3–13) the extent of the terror is developed in a series of images culminating in verses 11–13.

3–4. The fact that they sought darkness to hide sins is a reference to 14: 23 ('secret ceremonies'). The author considered this a new application of the basic thesis that man is punished by the very instrument by which he sinned (11: 16).

It is also a biblical idea to think that one can hide from God in the darkness. Nevertheless they could not escape and *lay in disorder*, separated from one another, while Israel assembled. *dreadfully afraid* and *terrified by apparitions* as in Ps. 78: 49: 'He loosed upon them the violence of his anger... launching those messengers of evil.'

5. *No fire...had force enough to give them light* suggests that the darkness was so oppressive that it put the fires out. Exod. 10: 21 says it could be 'felt'.

6. *a blaze, of no man's making*: not exactly in the biblical order since the phrase refers to the pillar of fire. The result, in any case, was to increase their terror.

7–10. *The tricks of the sorcerers' art failed* refers to Pharaoh's appeal to the magicians who at first had some success against Moses but ultimately failed. There is no reference in Exodus to the magicians trying to dispel darkness but again this is an example of the writer taking a liberty with the precise biblical text. *having once been scared* refers to the earlier plagues. Once fear set in there was no way to prevent its mounting intensity. And so *they collapsed in terror*. After all, the race had a curse on it from the beginning (12: 11).

11–13. *For* introduces the reason for such profound psychological fear. It was sin. Evil men, such as the Egyptians, under advantageous conditions, i.e. darkness, hide their wicked nature but when challenged by their own *conscience* become cowards. The word *conscience* appears here for the first time in the Septuagint but is frequent in the New Testament. The Greek word was common among the ethical writers of the first century B.C. and meant moral judgement, i.e. a second self standing over against the sinful self. Verse 12 leads on to say that *Fear* (or cowardice) destroys all reason. A guilty *conscience* disturbs any equilibrium that a man normally has. All hope is *defeated by this inward weakness* and man is unable to analyse the cause of the *torment*.

14. *So all that night, which really had no power against them...* *they slept*: darkness itself was harmless because it came from

the powerless depths of hell which is the place of death and
impotence (1: 14). *they slept* refers to the seventy-two-hour
house-arrest (verse 16, 'a prison that had no bars') imposed
upon the Egyptians by the darkness.

15. *now...now*: expresses the 'contrast' and accentuates
the degree of psychological anguish they experienced, *harried
by portentous spectres* and *paralysed by the treachery of their own
souls*.

17. *the same chain of darkness* bound all Egyptians wherever
and whoever they were.

18–19 list seven normal activities of nature which assume
monstrous proportions for the already terrified Egyptans.
The biblical source for these verses is Lev. 26: 36 'so ridden
with fear that, when a leaf flutters behind them in the
wind, they shall run'. The 'contrast' is accentuated by the
fact that all these natural phenomena, which under normal
conditions would be welcome, have now *paralysed them with
fear*.

20–1. *The whole world was bathed in the bright light of day*:
a reference to the Israelites who by contrast experienced 'no
darkness' wherever they lived (Exod. 10: 23). Verse 21 speaks
of the moral darkness falling upon Egypt (*heavier than the
darkness was the burden*). Furthermore, the darkness is the *image*
of what awaits them in death.   ✳

LIGHT FOR ISRAEL

✳ 18: 1–2. These verses refer to Exod. 10: 23 and resume the
idea already mentioned in 17: 20. The phrases *counted them
happy* and *gave thanks for their forbearance* are synonymous.
The Egyptians showered the fleeing Israelites with gifts.
Furthermore, the Egyptians were thankful that the Israelites
had not measured out comparable punishment (*lex talionis*)
on them for their years of suffering as slaves in Egypt.

3. *thy gift was a pillar of fire...a sun that would not scorch them*:
two parallel and synonymous phrases. Exod. 13: 21 speaks of

the pillar as a 'guide'. The Palestinian targum to Exod. 12: 37 speaks of the pillar as a protection against hail, rain, and the heat of the sun. The writer was perhaps suggesting that unlike the scorching heat of Sinai the pillar of fire was intended to light their way. Isa. 49: 10 says that 'no scorching heat or sun shall distress them'.

4. *Their enemies did indeed deserve*: the punishment fitted the crime (11: 16). They had imprisoned *thy sons*, who were God's agents bringing the *imperishable* ('incorrupt') *light of the law* to the world. These words provide a setting that is universal and for all eternity. The same perspective is found in Isa. 49: 6 'a light to the nations, to be my salvation to earth's farthest bounds'. The law is thought of here in its most comprehensive sense, including all divine revelation as the guide of life. Finally, the writer considered Egypt's suffering in the darkness very fitting punishment for depriving the world of the law's light. ✲

THE FIFTH 'CONTRAST' BETWEEN EGYPT AND ISRAEL: DEATH

5 They planned to kill the infant children of thy holy people, but when one child had been exposed to death and rescued, thou didst deprive them of all their children in requital, and drown them all together in the swelling 6 waves. Of that night our forefathers were given warning in advance, so that, having sure knowledge, they might 7 be heartened by the promises which they trusted. Thy people were looking for the deliverance of the godly and 8 the destruction of their enemies; for thou didst use the same means to punish our enemies and to make us glorious 9 when we heard thy call. The devout children of a virtuous race were offering sacrifices in secret, and covenanted with one consent to keep the law of God and to share alike

in the same blessings and the same dangers, and they were
already singing their sacred ancestral songs of praise. In 10
discordant contrast there came an outcry from their enemies, as piteous lamentation for their children spread
abroad. Master and slave were punished together with the 11
same penalty; king and common man suffered the same
fate. All alike had their dead, past counting, struck down 12
by one common form of death; there were not enough
living even to bury the dead; at one stroke the most
precious of their offspring had perished. Relying on their 13
magic arts, they had scouted all warnings; but when
they saw their first-born dead, they confessed that thy
people have God as their father.

All things were lying in peace and silence, and night in 14
her swift course was half spent, when thy almighty Word 15
leapt from thy royal throne in heaven into the midst of
that doomed land like a relentless warrior, bearing the 16
sharp sword of thy inflexible decree, and stood and filled
it all with death, his head touching the heavens, his feet
on earth. At once nightmare phantoms appalled them, 17
and unlooked-for fears set upon them; and as they flung 18
themselves to the ground half dead, one here, one there,
they confessed the reason for their deaths; for the dreams 19
that tormented them had caught them before they died,
so that they should not die ignorant of the reason why
they suffered.

The godly also had a taste of death when a multitude 20
were struck down in the wilderness; but the divine wrath
did not long continue. A blameless man was quick to be 21
their champion, bearing the weapons of his priestly
ministry, prayer and the incense that propitiates; he with-

stood the divine anger and set a limit to the disaster, thus
22 showing that he was thy servant. He overcame the
avenging fury not by bodily strength or force of arms; by
words he subdued the avenger, appealing to the sworn
23 covenants made with our forefathers. When the dead had
already fallen in heaps one on another, he interposed himself and beat back the divine wrath, barring its line of
24 attack upon the living. On his long-skirted robe the whole
world was represented; the glories of the fathers were
engraved on his four rows of precious stones; and thy
25 majesty was in the diadem upon his head. To these the
destroyer yielded, for these made him afraid; only to taste
his wrath had been enough.

✶ This 'contrast' is more complex in form and idea than the
others. Egypt is punished both by the death of her first-born
for slaying the Hebrew male children (Exod. 1: 16) and by
drowning in the Red Sea for having hurled the Hebrew male
babies into the Nile (Exod. 1: 22). Furthermore, the rescue of
one child was the cause for the wholesale destruction of
Egypt. Even though the idea of the Red Sea is broached here
it only finds full treatment in ch. 19. The idea of Moses as the
cause of Egypt's destruction is left undeveloped.

The key biblical verses which quite possibly lie at the base
of this fifth 'contrast' are Exod. 4: 22–3 '"Israel is my first-
born son. I have told you to let my son go, so that he may
worship me. You have refused to let him go, so I will kill
your first-born son."'

5–7. Extensive use is made of the Exodus narrative: *planned
to kill the infant children* (Exod. 1: 16); *one child...exposed...
rescued* (Exod. 2: 2–10); *deprive them of all their children in
requital* (Exod. 12: 19–30); *drown them* (Exod. 14: 26–9); *that
night*, i.e. 'the night of vigil' (Exod. 12: 42); *given warning*
(Exod. 11: 4–7). With the phrase *our forefathers* the writer

identified himself with the Israelites. In this book the term
applied to the Israelites in Egypt is *Thy people* (18: 7); therefore, *forefathers* most likely refers to the patriarchs to whom
deliverance from bondage was thought to have been revealed
according to Jewish tradition. The Palestinian targum to
Exod. 12: 42, commenting on the 'night of vigil', utilized an
ancient poem on 'The Four Nights' in Israel's history when
God had revealed himself as Israel's redeemer. The first night
was concerned with the creation of the world. 'The second
night: when the Lord was revealed to Abram...and Isaac...
The third night: when the Lord was revealed against the
Egyptians at midnight: his hand slew the first-born of the
Egyptians and his right hand protected the first-born of
Israel...The fourth night: when the world reached its end
to be redeemed...it is a night reserved and set aside for the
redemption of all the generations of Israel.' Such phrases as
*in advance, promises which they trusted, people were looking for the
deliverance*, and *destruction of their enemies* reflect the argument
of the targums.

8. *thou didst use the same means* (cp. 11: 16): in the following
verses (9–13) the contrasting reactions of the godly (verse 9)
and the ungodly (verses 10–13) to the terror of 'that night'
(verse 6) are described.

9. *devout children* is contrasted with 'children' of the
Egyptians in verse 10. *offering sacrifices in secret*: the Passover
was to be observed in the quiet of each Israelite home (Exod.
12: 46). *singing their sacred ancestral songs of praise* suggests the
unity of the people in *blessings* and *dangers*. Although there is
no evidence that the Hallel Psalms (songs of praise to God;
Pss. 113–18) were associated with the Passover in the exodus
period, it is possible that they were by the writer's time.

10–12. *In discordant contrast* is the enemies' outcry (Exod.
11: 6 'a great cry of anguish'). There is no distinction among
those receiving the punishment: *Master and slave were punished
together with the same penalty;...All alike had their dead* (cp.
Exod. 12: 29 'from the first-born of Pharaoh...to the first-

born of the captive in the dungeon'). The Palestinian targum to this verse in Exodus reads: 'from the first-born of Pharaoh ...to the sons of the kings who were captives in the dungeons as hostages and who, having rejoiced at the servitude of the Israelites, were punished as the Egyptians'. So total was the onslaught that *there were not enough living even to bury the dead* which seems to be an amplification of Num. 33: 3–4 which states that the Egyptians were still burying their dead even after the exodus had begun. *the most precious of their offspring* are the first-born (Ps. 105: 36 'the firstfruits of their manhood').

13. *they had scouted all warnings*: the various plagues sent by God which, at first, were successfully countered by magic (17: 7). Finally they were compelled to admit *God as their father* (i.e. the Israelites' father). In Exod. 4: 22–3 God said: 'Israel is my first-born son.' Hosea reasoned the same way (11: 1).

14–16. These verses contain a description of apocalyptic anger which in form may have been inspired by Job 4: 12–15 and in idea by 1 Chron. 21: 15–27. Job has: 'A word stole into my ears;...in the...night, when a man sinks into deepest sleep, terror seized me and shuddering.' Here, at midnight (*night in her swift course was half spent*; cp. Exod. 11: 4 and 12: 29, 'midnight') into this *peace and silence* the cataclysmic interruption took place: *thy almighty Word leapt...like a relentless warrior*. Among her many attributes wisdom is called 'all-powerful' (7: 23); the same Greek word is translated *almighty* here. The image of God as a warrior has already (5: 16–20; cp. 12: 9) been developed at some length by the writer. This warrior encompasses all: *his head touching the heavens, his feet on earth*. In 7: 24 wisdom 'pervades and permeates all things' while in 8: 1 'She spans the world in power from end to end'. It may be that 1 Chron. 21: 16 provided the writer with his imagery: 'When David looked up and saw the angel of the LORD standing between earth and heaven, with his sword drawn in his hand...' Also it is worth noting that a recently published targum fragment of Josh. 5: 13 for the phrase 'a man standing in front of him (Joshua) with a drawn sword' contains a description close to that in this book: 'and behold an angel whose name was Uriel; his height (was about from) the earth to the heaven and his breadth was about from Egypt to Jericho and in his hand was his sword drawn clear of the sheath'.

What is the meaning of *Word* in this passage? Although some scholars have suggested that *Word* has a Greek philosophical meaning we may determine the precise use by its other occurrences in Wisdom as well as its function in this chapter. Certainly there is no Greek overtone in the use of 'word' in 9: 1 where it is synonymous with 'wisdom'; 12: 9 ('one stern word'); 16: 12 ('all-healing word'); and 18: 22 ('by words he subdued'). In each of these passages it is an expression of the will of God in action, as in Ps. 147: 15, 18:

> He sends his command to the ends of the earth,
>   and his word runs swiftly...
> he utters his word, and the ice is melted.

Also, the whole spirit of ch. 18 is Hebraic rather than Greek.

The concept of both idea and action being inseparable in *Word* is Hebraic. Here *Word* is linked with action: the *Word leapt* and is personified as *a relentless warrior*.

The direct Old Testament reference is 1 Chron. 21: 15 where the angel of the Lord is God's agent of destruction. But the ministry of angels has no place in Wisdom. Therefore, God is personified as 'wisdom', 'word', etc. Also in the Palestinian targum to Exod. 12: 29 it is 'the word of the Lord' which 'slew the first-born'. The personification of God as 'wisdom' or 'word' in no way suggests that *Word* has a role independent of God. Jewish theology, in attempting to modify the transcendental reality of God, did not formulate a second God. For *thy almighty Word* one can substitute 'God' without altering the meaning of the verse. In conclusion, the *Word* is used as a poetic personification of God's will and action (cp. Isa. 55: 11 'so shall the word which comes from my mouth prevail').

The fact that the N.E.B. capitalizes *Word* in this phrase and nowhere else in the text of Wisdom suggests that the translators considered this passage to have significance beyond the limits of the book (cp. John 1: 1–14 where 'word' is also capitalized: 'the Word already was').

17–19. *At once nightmare phantoms appalled them*: what follows has no biblical basis. The description underlines the intensity of the fear which overpowered the Egyptians (ch. 17). *should not die ignorant of the reason why they suffered*: not only did those who survived recognize God's power (verse 13) but the first-born also (verse 19). The writer was anxious that all should understand the full meaning of the judgement.

20. The argument of verses 20–5 is consistent with that in the preceding 'contrast'. Israel only had to 'taste' God's wrath (verse 25; cp. 16: 5) in order to know how much more grievous was the punishment of Egypt. *a taste of death*: the plague which struck Israel (Num. 16: 45 'Stand well clear of this community, so that in a single instant I may make an end of them') was because of the sin of Korah, Dathan, and Abiram. God's anger did not continue long, in contrast to the 'pitiless anger' with which he pursued the godless 'to the bitter end' (19: 1).

21–3. *A blameless man*: Aaron. For the details related to this section note Num. 16: 46–8 where Aaron goes before the people with his censer to mitigate the plague which had struck them. The reason for Aaron, rather than Moses, is his priestly office. This tradition about Aaron is already old in this book if we consider similar ideas in other contemporary writings. In the Palestinian targum it is Aaron who is 'a pillar for Israel because he is the one who makes expiation for them once a year'. *by words he subdued the avenger*: i.e. prayer; but the author may also be recalling 'the almighty Word' (verse 15). *the avenger*: the destroying angel recorded in 1 Chron. 21: 15 and so the one to be subdued. *appealing to the sworn covenants* (cp. 12: 21; 18: 6, 9): those agreements of the past

provide hope in this moment. Possibly also the writer thought
of Exod. 32: 13 'I will make your posterity countless.'

24–5. The conquest was not by strength but by the words
of Aaron the priest who was wearing his priestly robes. That
robe was blue and so depicted *the whole world*. The names of
the twelve patriarchs (*glories of the fathers*) were written on
the precious stones which encrusted the breast-plate. On the
diadem was inscribed 'Holy to the Lord' (*majesty*). *To these*:
to the high priest, clothed in his robes, the fathers, and God
before whom *the destroyer*, that is 'the avenger' (verse 22),
yielded. In 5: 17ff. the same imagery was used to demonstrate
the power of God as a warrior against the enemy of 'the just'. ✲

THE SIXTH 'CONTRAST' BETWEEN EGYPT AND
ISRAEL: THE RED SEA

But the godless were pursued by pitiless anger to the **19**
bitter end, for God knew their future also: how after 2
allowing thy people to depart, and even urging their
departure, they would change their minds and set out in
pursuit. While they were still mourning, still lamenting 3
at the graves of their dead, they rushed into another
foolish decision, and pursued as fugitives those whom they
had begged to leave. For the fate they had merited was 4
drawing them on to this conclusion and made them forget
what had happened, so that they might suffer the torments
still needed to complete their punishment, and that thy 5
people might achieve an incredible journey, and that their
enemies might meet an outlandish death.

The whole creation, with all its elements, was re- 6
fashioned in subservience to thy commands, so that thy
servants might be preserved unscathed. Men gazed at the 7
cloud that overshadowed the camp, at dry land emerging

where before was only water, at an open road leading out
of the Red Sea, and a grassy plain in place of stormy waves,
8 across which the whole nation passed, under the shelter
9 of thy hand, after all the marvels they had seen. They were
like horses at pasture, like skipping lambs, as they praised
10 thee, O Lord, by whom they were rescued. For they still
remembered their life in a foreign land: how instead of
cattle the earth bred lice, and instead of fish the river
11 spewed up swarms of frogs; and how, after that, they had
seen a new sort of bird when, driven by greed, they had
12 begged for delicacies to eat, and for their relief quails
came up from the sea.

13 So punishment came upon those sinners, not un-
heralded by violent thunderbolts. They suffered justly for
their own wickedness, for they had raised bitter hatred of
14 strangers to a new pitch. There had been others who
refused to welcome strangers when they came to them,
but these made slaves of guests who were their bene-
15 factors. There is indeed a judgement awaiting those who
16 treated foreigners as enemies; but these, after a festal welcome, oppressed with hard labour men who had earlier
17 shared their rights. They were struck with blindness also,
like the men at the door of the one good man, when
yawning darkness fell upon them and each went groping
for his own doorway.

18 For as the notes of a lute can make various tunes with
different names though each retains its own pitch, so the
elements combined among themselves in different ways,
as can be accurately inferred from the observation of what
19 happened. Land animals took to the water and things that
20 swim migrated to dry land; fire retained its normal power

even in water, and water forgot its quenching properties. Flames on the other hand failed to consume the flesh of 21 perishable creatures that walked in them, and the substance of heavenly food, like ice and prone to melt, no longer melted.

✻ 1–2. Because God knew that the Egyptians, having 'begged' (verse 3) Israel to go, would regret it and pursue them (Exod. 14: 6 'So Pharaoh put horses to his chariot, and took his troops with him'), therefore the Egyptians were *pursued by pitiless anger to the bitter end.* In 12: 10 God's punishment of the godless was carried out gradually to allow room for repentance. Here, in contrast, because God knew *their future* wilfulness he did not check his anger.

3. *rushed into another foolish decision* suggests that the Egyptians had not learned from their experience. Instead, they decided to pursue the Israelites assuming, according to Exod. 14: 2, that the Israelites would find 'themselves in difficult country' and so be easily re-taken.

4. *the fate they had merited* is the inevitable consequence of cause and effect. The author was not thinking of fate in the predetermined sense. Verse 13 expresses it well: 'They suffered justly for their own wickedness.' *forget what had happened*: i.e. the plagues and the death of their first-born. This inevitable folly dulled their senses so that they did not remember the terrible events already experienced. *the torments still needed to complete their punishment* reflects the thinking that to punish the impious directly is an act of kindness. 2 Macc. 6: 14 notes 'with them (the Gentiles) he patiently holds his hand until they have reached the full extent of their sins'. In contrast, God inflicted punishment upon his own people before their sins had reached their height. If the Egyptians could have remembered the plagues they would have checked themselves. God gave them enough rope to hang themselves.

5. This underlines the 'contrast': the *incredible journey* of

Israel through the wilderness (cp. 18: 3 'their uncharted journey') guided by the pillar of fire; the *outlandish death* of the Egyptians in the water of the Red Sea.

6. The reaction of Israel and Egypt to the Red Sea experience is the next topic undertaken: verses 6–12 offer an imaginative account of the Israelite reaction to that experience; verses 13–17 recount the punishment visited upon the Egyptians.

The whole creation...was refashioned: *creation* (here, as in 5: 17; 16: 24) means nature. The miracle of the Red Sea is explained in philosophical language as the mutual exchange of elements. Nothing new came into being when a miracle occurred. Later, this thesis is explained in terms of musical notes and various tunes (verse 18). The reason for the refashioning of nature is stated: *so that thy servants might be preserved unscathed*. Therefore, verse 6 is stating in a philosophical way the thesis underlying chs. 11 and 16–19 – that the 'selfsame means' by which an oppressor is punished becomes a blessing to the oppressed (11: 5) and that 'the instruments of a man's sin are the instruments of his punishment' (11: 16).

7–9. These verses contain the author's description of the passage through the Red Sea. Some of the details are biblical (*cloud*, Exod. 13: 21–2; *dry land*, Exod. 14: 16) while others seem to be drawn from an interpretative source such as the Palestinian targum to Exod. 15: 19: 'The children of Israel went through on dry land in the midst of the sea; on the bottom of the sea were food, trees, herbs, and delicacies.' Such phrases as *cloud*, *shelter of thy hand* indicate the continued protection of God. The phrase *they praised thee, O Lord, by whom they were rescued* reflects the joy felt by Israel in the song of Miriam in Exod. 15. The simile *like horses* is Isaiah's description (63: 13): 'causing them to go through the depths sure-footed as horses in the wilderness'.

10. *still remembered*: the Red Sea experience underlines the contrast between this blessing and the suffering of the Egyptians. In 16: 11 the author told us that the serpents were sent

to remind the people of God's utterances. The term *bred* must be understood in the sense of Exod. 8: 17: 'All the dust turned into maggots throughout the land of Egypt.' *bred* is used in a pejorative sense and is parallel in meaning to *the river spewed up*.

11–12. *a new sort of bird*: the emphasis on *new sort* is not that the quail was a unique bird previously unknown but rather that its extraordinary quality and continuous supply were new phenomena. *quails came up from the sea* seems to reflect Num. 11: 31 'from the west' and also the writer's imagination. Furthermore, he drew from Ps. 105: 40: 'They asked, and he sent them quails, he gave them bread from heaven in plenty.'

13–17. In contrast to the kindness shown by God to the Israelites in the preceding verses, *those sinners*, the Egyptians, received their deserved punishment, which took place amidst *violent thunderbolts*. Already in 5: 20ff. all nature was used by God 'against his frenzied foes'. Ps. 77: 17–19 records the same idea:

> The clouds poured water, the skies thundered,
>> thy arrows flashed hither and thither.
> The sound of thy thunder was in the whirlwind,
>> thy lightnings lit up the world.

In the Palestinian targum to Exod. 14: 24 we find the same tradition: 'the word of the Lord looked forth upon the host of the Egyptians and cast upon them pitch and fire and hail-stones'. The Egyptians *suffered justly* because *they raised bitter hatred of strangers to a new pitch*. The Egyptians are compared to the inhospitable Sodomites in the following verses. The writer continued to avoid the use of proper names but there is every reason to believe that *others who refused to welcome strangers* were the men of Sodom as recorded in Gen. 19. Here, how-ever, it is suggested that the Egyptians were more inhospitable. The reason becomes clear in the following comparison. Firstly, the Egyptians *made slaves of guests who were their benefactors*. The Israelites had been invited to come to Egypt according to Gen. 45: 17–18: 'Fetch your father...I will give you the best that there is in Egypt.' Israel had been Egypt's *benefactors* through her illustrious ancestor Joseph and also because of the service rendered during the years of captivity. Secondly, the Israelites, *after a festal welcome* (Gen. 45: 17–20), were *oppressed with hard labour*. And this, despite the fact that they had civil *rights*. This last statement may well be an exaggeration but could be supported from Gen. 45: 18 – 'I will give you the best.'

To a degree the author held the Sodomites less culpable because they treated *foreigners as enemies* from the beginning. They did not add fickleness to their crimes. However, *There is indeed a judgement awaiting* Sodom.

The Egyptians *were struck with blindness*, which is a reference to the plague of darkness. Likewise the men of Sodom (Gen. 19: 11: 'they struck the men in the doorway with blindness'). The *yawning darkness* which fell on the land of Egypt (Exod. 10: 21–3) made the Egyptians 'prisoners of darkness and captives of unending night...each immured under his own roof' (17: 2; see also 17: 17). The contrast is between the Sodomites who lost their sight and the Egyptians who were deprived of light. The *one good man* is Lot (cp. 10: 6). In Gen. 19: 9–10 the Sodomites sought to break down the door to Lot's house in an attempt to destroy him. There is no reference in Gen. 19 to the men of Sodom looking for their *own doorway* and this last phrase may well refer back to the plight of the Egyptians in the darkness. If so, then even within verse 17 the writer contrasts the actions of the Sodomites and the Egyptians

18–21. These verses summarize the thinking of the author of Wisdom. He has already stated his thesis in theological terms in 11: 5, the means for punishment and blessing are the same, and 11: 16, the instruments of sin become the instruments of punishment. In verse 18 the writer drew on the Greek philosophical theory that elements could be interchanged, to express his biblical bias. What God did for Israel in the exodus is a miracle. God took *the elements* and shaped them in an orderly way. That was the first tune. Then God combined *the elements* in *different ways* (cp. 19: 6 'The whole creation... was refashioned') and there was a new tune, although the notes remained the same. And this can be *inferred from the observation of what happened* as cited in chs. 11 and 16–19. The fact that these miraculous events took place occasioned no disorder, nor interfered with the harmony of the cosmos, any more than the transposing of a melody.

Verses 19–21 discuss, in summary and therefore somewhat repetitiously, the theory expressed in verse 18 concerning land, water, and fire. *Land animals*: with the Israelites passing through the Red Sea 'went a large company of every kind, and cattle in great numbers, both flocks and herds' (Exod. 12: 38). *things that swim*: the frogs. Furthermore, verse 20 repeats the argument of 16: 16–17. Verse 21 repeats 16: 18 concerning 'the living creatures inflicted on the godless' and 16: 22 in describing the manna as 'snow and ice'. ✶

GOD, EVERYMAN'S HELPER

In everything, O Lord, thou hast made thy people great 22
and glorious, and hast not neglected in every time and
place to be their helper.

✶ There is nothing left for the author to say. The verse sums up in a theological vein (in contrast to verse 18's philosophical tone) the thesis which the writer has been propounding in his restatement of the meaning of the exodus wanderings, that is, God is constantly (*hast not neglected*) the *helper* of his chosen people, no matter what trial or tribulation they suffer, and makes them *great and glorious. in every time and place* contemporizes the whole recitation of Israel's history. If God did help Israel in the exodus he will and can still help the Jews of Egypt in the writer's day. ✶

✶   ✶   ✶   ✶   ✶   ✶   ✶   ✶   ✶   ✶   ✶   ✶   ✶

WHY READ WISDOM TODAY?

The hellenistic Jew to whom the book was addressed was much attracted to all the variety, sophistication, and excitement that hellenism seemed to be able to offer. It must have been a fantastic world in which the writer of Wisdom lived. In art, learning, literature, and engineering there had never been anything like it before.

The problem which confronted the writer was how to make the Bible relevant to his contemporaries. In the first place he took seriously the secular culture in which they were living and made use of it to demonstrate the deeper and more universal value of God's concern for man. In other words, he presented a third dimension to man's daily life. This end was achieved by using the literary style with which everyone was familiar, to express the truth about God as revealed in the Bible. Instead of merely employing traditional methods of explaining the biblical text, he brought the Bible into everyday life and applied to it the current literary and philosophical arguments.

The writer of the book argued skilfully for the continuing validity of the Jewish faith in the face of this cultural challenge. The book he produced is a model of how to make the ancient scriptures meaningful and relevant to a later generation.

The questions of man's relationship to God and God's place in the ongoing life of the world as well as man's purpose for living are as relevant today as they were in the writer's time. His conviction was that in every age there is need for stability. God is that anchor. Paul, for instance, stated the same conviction: 'and in everything, as we know, he (God) co-operates for good with those who love God and are called according to his purpose' (Rom. 8: 28). The writer of Wisdom reminded his fellow-Jews of God's loyalty in the exodus and argued that God would not neglect any man who gets wisdom in this crisis of faith. Paul says that it is the spirit which man needs to help him overcome his weakness.

Why read Wisdom today?

Today we are faced with the same fundamental universal questions about life and its meaning. The cultural challenge and pressures which surround us are much the same but in different dress. Alone we are unable to survive the crisis. With God (wisdom) we can begin to win the battle of life.

☆   ☆   ☆   ☆   ☆   ☆   ☆   ☆   ☆   ☆   ☆   ☆

A NOTE ON FURTHER READING

For some additional reading to fill in the background to the age in which the writer lived read: F. E. Peters, *The Harvest of Hellenism* (New York, 1970) and D. S. Russell, *The Jews from Alexander to Herod* (Oxford, 1967). For the extent of hellenistic influence on the writer and how he used it rather than compromise his Jewish faith, consult J. M. Reese, *Hellenistic Influence on the Book of Wisdom and its Consequences* (Rome, 1970). For an overall view of wisdom literature in the Old Testament, consult R. B. Y. Scott, *The Way of Wisdom* (New York, 1971; London, 1972) and William McKane, *Proverbs* (London, 1970). The older commentary on *Wisdom* by J. A. F. Gregg (Cambridge, 1909) is still worth consulting.

INDEX

133